American Mythology

DON NARDO

LUCENT BOOKS
A part of Gale, Cengage Learning

GALE
CENGAGE Learning

Detroit • New York • San Francisco • New Haven, Conn • Waterville, Maine • London

LIBRARY OF CONGRESS CATALOGING-IN-PUBLICATION DATA

Nardo, Don, 1947-
 American mythology / by Don Nardo.
   p. cm. -- (Mythology and culture worldwide)
 Includes bibliographical references and index.
 ISBN 978-1-4205-0904-5
 1. United States--Folklore--Juvenile literature. 2. Tales--United States--Juvenile literature. 3. Legends--United States--Juvenile literature. I. Title.
 GR105.N36 2013
 398.20973--dc23
                                                    2012033859

Lucent Books
27500 Drake Rd.
Farmington Hills, MI 48331

ISBN-13: 978-1-4205-0904-5
ISBN-10: 1-4205-0904-7

Printed in the United States of America
2 3 4 5 6 7 16 15 14 13

TABLE OF CONTENTS

American Myth Locator Map

Paul Bunyan

Sea Serpent
of 1877

Phantom Puppies

Johnny
Appleseed

Ringwood Manor

Mothman

Blackbeard's
Ghost

Hairy Man

Flying Dutchman

Major Characters in American Mythology

Character Name	Description
Babe the Blue Ox	An enormous ox who became the faithful companion of the famous lumberjack Paul Bunyan. It was said that Babe was so strong he could pull the curves out of a winding road.
Bigfoot	A large, hairy, apelike beast that people claim to have seen in remote, forested areas of the American Northwest (as well as other places around the globe).
Blackbeard's Ghost	The restless spirit of the mean-spirited pirate Edward Teach, better known as Blackbeard. Headless, the zombie-like phantom relentlessly searches for Teach's lost treasure.
Bogeyman	A monster who supposedly steals small children.
Captain Sandovate	The common name for Don Sandovate, a legendary ship captain who searched for treasure in the Americas. His crew mutinied, stole his treasure, and then tied him to a mast and left him to die.
Hairy Man	One of several manifestations of the dreaded Bogeyman, the Hairy Man is said to live in a swamp somewhere in the Appalachian Mountains. He hunts for little children.
Jersey Devil	A frightening, flying creature that is said to terrorize people in and near the forests of New Jersey's Pine Barrens.
John Henry	A renowned nineteenth-century African American railroad worker. He is most famous for taking part in a contest with a machine to determine which could hammer the most railroad spikes the fastest.
Johnny Appleseed	The nickname for John Chapman, a mild-mannered man born shortly before the start of the American Revolution. He is known for planting apple trees across large sections of the Midwest.
Mothman	A fearsome flying creature that a number of people in southwestern West Virginia claimed to have seen during the 1960s and 1970s. Some suggested that it caused a local bridge collapse that killed several people.
Paul Bunyan	The famous super-sized logger who, with his companion Babe the Blue Ox, was said to roam the woodlands of the northern United States, cutting down huge swaths of trees with a single swing of his immense ax.

Pecos Bill	An oversize, incredibly energetic cowboy who was raised by coyotes and actually thought he was a coyote until he found out he was really a human being. Legend says he performed numerous fantastic feats, including riding a tornado like it was a bucking bronco.
Sasquatch	The name given to each member of a group of large, hairy, apelike beasts that some people claim to have seen in remote, forested areas of the American Northwest (as well as other places around the globe).
Sea Serpent of 1817	Perhaps the best-known sea monster to terrorize the U.S. eastern seaboard, the massive creature was also sighted along the shores of New York's Long Island.
Werewolves of Detroit	These part-man, part-wolf creatures were in colonial times said to infest the region around Detroit, Michigan, then an important frontier outpost.
Zorro	The secret identity of Don Diego de la Vega, a legendary Spanish-speaking nobleman who had a large ranch in Southern California before it became a U.S. state. Zorro, or "the Fox," supposedly helped local citizens who were oppressed by corrupt government authorities.

Teaching People About Themselves

After the American frontier figure Davy Crockett died in the siege of the Alamo in March 1836, his name became forever associated with that noted event. Along with fellow frontiersman Jim Bowie and a few others, he is still remembered as a hero who gave his life to liberate Texas from the tyranny of the Mexican dictator Santa Anna. There was nothing mythological about that aspect of Crockett's bigger-than-life image. He earned the right to be called a hero by taking part in a real, well-documented event.

Yet Crockett was already widely seen as an American frontier hero well before he arrived at the Alamo, and for very different reasons. He was born in obscure circumstances in the late 1700s in the backwoods of what is now Tennessee. But as a young man, he became involved in high-profile activities such as fighting under future president Andrew Jackson in wars against the Creek Indians and successfully running for the U.S. Congress.

Crockett loved telling stories, especially tall tales, and was very good at it. So he learned to use his real, colorful achievements as a springboard to further fame and regularly beefed up his résumé with fictitious accomplishments. Either he or newspaper reporters and other writers seeking to increase their readership spun all sorts of exaggerated or fabricated accounts of his adventures. Typical was the story that he had killed a full-grown bear when he was just three years old.

In this way a mythology of considerable proportions grew up around Crockett's name and image, both in his own lifetime and after his death. He became an American folk hero on a par with some highly popular frontier characters, some of whom were never real people in the first place. Among their illustrious number were Paul Bunyan, supposedly a huge, incredibly strong lumberjack; John Henry, an African American railroad worker with unmatched strength and determination; Pecos Bill, a sort of supercowboy; and Zorro, a gallant masked defender of oppressed peasants in early Spanish American California.

Other Kinds of Tall Tales

The stories about these and other legendary figures associated with the United States' formative years were not the only myths propagated in that period. The earliest of all the American legends were those describing mythical and mystical lost cities. The first Spanish, Portuguese, English, and other European explorers and adventurers who landed in the so-called New World were fascinated by tales of cities with streets and buildings made of gold. Supposedly, these and the imposing kingdoms they were a part of lay somewhere in the vast, unexplored wilderness of the Americas.

Still other kinds of myths emerged as the first European settlements began to spring up in North America, including the future United States. The Europeans who established those initially small and rustic villages and towns brought with them many of the superstitions and tall tales they had collected in their native lands. These included legends of ghosts, werewolves, lake monsters, and the like.

The frontier wilderness that confronted these early settlers was enormous, largely unknown, and to some degree frightening. So there was every reason to believe that it, like the more remote areas of Europe, held its share of weird creatures and supernatural forces. Over time, therefore, many folktales and myths developed about American monsters on the loose and ghosts that haunted the living. (Folktales are a kind of myth used primarily to entertain; other myths do that but also teach people moral lessons and other things.)

Relating Humans to Nature

Whatever the type or nature of American myths, in large degree they came to reflect the beliefs, customs, and aspirations of the ordinary folk who populated the infant country. Almost all of these settlers were devoutly religious as well as superstitious. So they strongly believed in the doctrine that people who committed various sins would surely receive their just punishments. That divine retribution, or punishment from God, might take any number of forms, including offbeat and scary ones. As a result, a number of the early myths involving ghosts and monsters depicted those creatures seeking out and penalizing criminals and other guilty persons.

Myths about heroes were generated in a similar manner. It took much strength and courage to go out into the unexplored wilderness and carve out farms and towns. So the early European settlers greatly admired mythical frontier heroes like Paul Bunyan, who displayed those same laudable attributes. Circulating stories about such characters was a way for average settlers to draw attention to and take pride in their own difficult achievements. One modern observer elaborates, using the giant lumberjack as an example:

> The wild frontier challenged the American people. Yet, through perseverance and sheer effort, nature was conquered. In order to create the frontier spirit, various folk heroes were born in our imaginations in order to embody the vitality of frontier life. . . . This gigantic man, who could chop down whole forests with a sweep of his ax, is one aspect of the frontier spirit. Constantly working on harvesting lumber for the new settlers, this tireless worker never stopped widening the frontier. Nature may have been wild and large, [and] seemingly unconquerable, but this tale of a man bigger than nature gave hope to the settlers. Man [that is, humanity] was bigger and stronger than his opponents [the natural elements], and he would persevere.[1]

American lumberjacks of the Pacific Northwest take a break to pose for a photo. Lumberjacks' stories of Paul Bunyan were a way to draw attention to and take pride in their own difficult achievements in carving out a civilization from the wilderness.

Myths Are Permanent

Thus, the earliest Americans dealt with sin, divine retribution, fear of the unknown, strength, and courage on a regular basis. They also worked hard to tame the wilderness in order to forge new lives and a better fate for themselves. These were only some of the concepts and problems they wrestled with, and whatever bothered, challenged, scared, or inspired them seems to have been reflected in one or more folktales and myths.

Moreover, these tales did not fade away over time. Instead, people kept the tales alive, and as new ones appeared, they became part of a growing collection of stories that passed from one generation to the next. This body of mythical Americana, so to speak, is as fulsome and fascinating today as it was to past generations. The late, widely respected American literary critic Gilbert Highet explained why. "Myths are permanent," he pointed out.

> They deal with the greatest of all problems, which do not change, because men and women do not change. They deal with love; with war; with sin; with tyranny; with courage; with fate; and all in some way or other deal with the relation of [humanity] to those divine powers which are sometimes felt to be irrational, sometimes to be cruel, and sometimes, alas, to be just.[2]

People create myths as a means of examining and dealing with their own desires, fears, and moral choices. Admirable characters like John Henry and Zorro became role models to look up to and imitate; legends of golden cities tested human gullibility and revealed the pitfalls of greed; and mythical monsters and ghosts reflected people's darker side, which many felt needed to be faced and overcome. In these ways American myths have helped to identify and shape who the American people are. Beyond their sheer entertainment value, the power of these stories is their ability to help people and society recognize their challenges and overcome them, or to recognize their faults and seek to improve on them.

CHAPTER 1

Legendary Lost Cities

S tories about mysterious lost cities have captured people's imaginations throughout recorded history. Some were long thought to be imaginary but were later found to be real places that had fallen into ruin and disappeared from view. Among the better-known examples are Troy and Leifsbudir. Troy was the city sacked by the ancient Greeks in the ancient Greek poet Homer's epic poem the *Iliad*. The city was assumed to be legendary, until a German archaeologist discovered its remains in an earthen mound in northwestern Turkey in the 1870s.

Similarly, in 1960 the Vikings' North American colony of Leifsbudir was unearthed at L'Anse aux Meadows in northern Newfoundland. Likely in the same category is Aztlán, the legendary original home of the Aztecs, the Native American people who once controlled much of Central America. A number of modern scholars think Aztlán may have been real and might someday be uncovered somewhere in the southern or western United States.

In contrast, other legendary lost cities were long thought by some people to be possibly real but were eventually shown to be only mythical. Some well-known examples in this category include El Dorado in South America, the Seven Cities of Cibola in the western United States, and Atlantis (also described as a large island) in what is now the Atlantic Ocean not far off North America's coast. These imaginary lost cities had or in many cases still have a genuine air of mystery surrounding them, along with a sense of nostalgia for wondrous times past. Such qualities have stirred people of all walks of life to speculate about their possible locations and what they looked like. As researchers Jennifer Westwood and James Harpur put it, they "are eternal realms whose fabled existence has inspired poets, painters, and scholars. [They feature] landscapes imbued with a divine spirit . . . sacred ruins ennobled by their settings, monuments of man, the fruit of his creative imagination, and shrines which testify to the indomitable human spirit."[3]

Some of history's most renowned fabled lost cities and civilizations were said to be located in the Americas. A majority of these supposedly existed in what is now the continental United States. In fact, compelling tales about these places were a major factor in drawing many of the earliest European explorers to American shores. In addition, these tales became the first examples of a trove of folklore and myths specifically identified with the lands of the future United States and the peoples who settled it.

An Enchanted Paradise?

The location of the fabulous Seven Cities of Cibola, or Seven Cities of Gold, was the earliest mystery associated with what late medieval Europeans called the New World. Spain was in the forefront of the European nations that scrambled to explore and profit from these faraway, unknown lands. Of the many Spaniards who searched for the Seven Cities, the most famous was explorer Francisco Vásquez de Coronado. Not long after his birth in 1510, he first heard the fascinating tale of these cities, which were said to contain vast amounts of gold and other valuables.

Although European knowledge of the Americas was fairly new when Coronado was a child, the tale of the Seven Cities of Cibola was not. The story had been generated some seven centuries before, in the period in which Muslim armies swept across North Africa. Some of these conquerors crossed the Strait of Gibraltar and entered the Iberian Peninsula, now composed of Spain and Portugal.

Most of the natives in the area were Christians, and some of them attempted to escape the intruders. According to the tale of the Seven Cities, one group of escapees fled around A.D. 1000. Among their number were seven Christian bishops and their disciples. They boarded their ships and sailed out into the Atlantic, hoping to find a land of refuge in that still unexplored watery realm. Eventually, the story goes, they did find an uncharted land beyond the western horizon. There each of the seven bishops erected a large city and over time filled it with gold and other riches collected from across that fruitful, enchanted paradise.

A period map shows the route of Spanish explorer Francisco Vásquez de Coronado through the Southwest in his expedition to find the legendary Seven Cities of Gold in 1540.

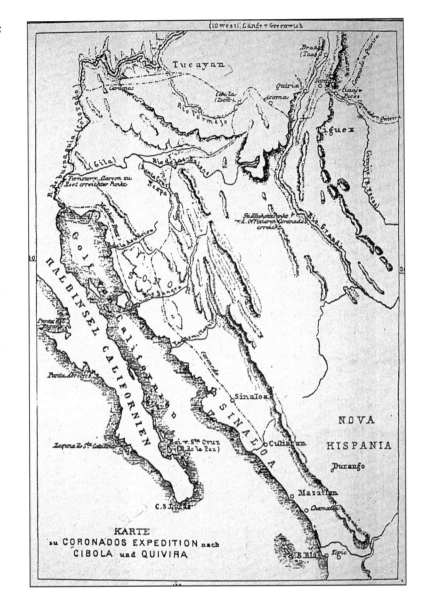

Some Europeans viewed this story as a mere tall tale, but many did not. The latter came to believe that there might well be some truth to it. The problem was that for a long time no one dared to mount a major expedition to see what lay on the far side of the ocean. The general consensus was that those waters contained giant monsters or other dangers that spelled certain death.

Then in 1492 the Italian explorer Christopher Columbus demonstrated that previously unknown lands *did* exist in the midst of the Atlantic. Sailing for the Spanish monarchy, he made multiple voyages to the West Indies, the islands in what is now called the Caribbean Sea. Other explorers followed him. They showed that the so-called Americas were made up not simply of small islands but also of entire new continents even bigger than Europe.

Motives for Seeking Gold

Those who believed the old story of the Seven Cities was true, among them the young Coronado, became convinced that they were located somewhere in the Americas. Moreover, they were sure that whoever was first to find them would become rich. Yet it was not just the desire for personal wealth that drove these individuals. The quest for the golden cities and the myth itself was part of a much larger set of cultural realities that then existed. Indeed, this was a classic case of a myth that both reflected and intensified certain accepted beliefs, customs, and social values.

First, at that time the economies of Spain, Portugal, and Europe's other leading nations were in large degree dependent on gold, silver, and other valuables. Those countries that could amass the most gold and other precious commodities could afford to raise the biggest armies and navies. In turn, these forces could be used either to intimidate or conquer neighboring countries. So the richest nations were almost always the most powerful and successful. Therefore, when the Americas were discovered and the existence of cities filled with gold appeared to be probable, acquiring that gold became a national priority of some European governments.

On a more personal level, soldier-adventurers like Coronado, men the Spanish called conquistadores, did desire to find that gold in order to

De Soto's Quest for Gold

Coronado was not the only Spanish conquistador who searched for the Seven Cities. Another was Hernando de Soto, who began looking about the same time as Friar Marcos did. De Soto never found the lost cities, but he became the first European to see the Mississippi River.

become rich. However, this was only part of what motivated them. They also wanted to increase their social and/or political status, and they could do this by providing their country with new sources of wealth. Any man who greatly enriched the Spanish national treasury, for example, could expect to be made a general, to receive various noble titles, and to hob-nob with royalty for the rest of his days.

The Great Expedition

These were the motives that drove the adult Coronado to search for the Seven Cities. His opportunity appeared after he moved to Spain's largest American colony, New Spain, encompassing much of what is now Mexico. There he got to know the Spanish governor, called the viceroy, Antonio de Mendoza. Like other Spaniards, Mendoza had long been obsessed with the idea of finding the seven golden cities. To that end, in 1539 he had sent a priest named Marcos de Niza to search for the cities in the unexplored regions lying north of New Spain. This enormous area would much later become a prosperous nation—the United States.

After a few months, Niza had returned to New Spain with promising news. Several of the American Indians he had met on his journey claimed that some cities lay farther north, in the continent's interior. Moreover, the people who dwelled in those cities regularly traded gold and other valuables. This report excited Mendoza. He believed it was strong evidence for the existence of the Seven Cities and that mounting a full-scale expedition to reach the cities was warranted.

To lead this important mission, the viceroy chose none other than his close and trusted friend Coronado. Eager to get started, the two men assembled a large number of Spaniards and local Indians in February 1540. In the words of the expedition's historian, Pedro de Castañeda, who kept a log of the trip, "More than 300 Spaniards and about 800 natives of New Spain collected in a few days. There were so many men of such high quality among the Spaniards, that such a noble body was never collected in the Indies, nor so many men of quality in such a small body. . . . Francisco Vazquez de Coronado [was] captain-general."[4]

Coronado and his lieutenants set out with their army into what is now the southwestern United States with great hopes of finding the Seven Cities and the riches they were said to contain. These hopes were further enhanced when the expedition encountered an Indian who claimed he knew about the cities. They called him the Turk, because his dark skin reminded them of the complexions of some North African peoples that many Europeans called Turks. The Indians called the cities Quivira, the Turk said. According to a modern expert on the American West, the Indian

Coronado's conquistadors were not only motivated by dreams of untold wealth but also the need to improve their social status.

> began to unfold exciting stories about Quivira, those incredible Indian cities lying far to the north across the plains. Set in a beautiful, level country, they bordered

a river two leagues [5.2 miles or 8.4km] wide, filled with fish as big as horses. Over its surface sped great canoes with twenty rowers to a side, the tribal sachems [chiefs] taking their ease under canopies sheltering raised decks at the rear. While bolting down thick, juicy slabs of buffalo flesh, the Spaniards listened attentively as the weaver of tales described the lord of this country, who took his afternoon nap beneath trees hung with golden bells which, when stirred by the breeze, lulled him to sleep. Why, even the dishes and water jugs of the common folk were of solid gold![5]

Despite the Turk's apparent certainty about the fabulous cities, Coronado never found them. He discovered seemingly endless rolling plains, giant herds of buffalo, and many Indian villages and huts, but no golden cities. Believing that the Turk had lied to him, he had the man executed. Modern experts think that, indeed, the Turk and other Indians who claimed to know of large cities lying far away *were* lying. Their motivation in doing so was to convince the Spaniards to keep going and leave their local villages alone and intact. The golden cities, it turned out, were never anything more than a myth. Still, like many other Spaniards of his era, Coronado never gave up his belief that they were real. "Somewhere beyond the sunrise," he purportedly declared as an old man, "I know for a certainty that a golden city lies!"[6]

El Dorado and La Canela

Coronado, Mendoza, and other Spaniards who settled in what is now Mexico had attempted to institute a national policy that eventually came to be neatly summarized by the words *God*, *glory*, and *gold*. Here, *God* referred to the goal of converting the non-Christian natives of the Americas to Christianity. *Glory* translated as the enhanced prestige Spain would acquire thanks to its rapidly expanding global empire. *Gold*, of course, was shorthand for the riches the Spanish hoped to accumulate in the Americas. Some of this would no doubt be found among the local natives, Spanish leaders believed. But much more might come from the discovery of fabulously wealthy lost cities.

Coronado's Sad Tidings to the King

After extensive searches that took him through large sections of the American West and Midwest, including Arizona, Oklahoma, and Kansas, Coronado reluctantly and sadly concluded that the legendary cities of gold did not exist. It was not merely a matter of personal disappointment. He had promised the Spanish king, Charles V, that he would locate the Seven Cities, which meant that he now had to explain to that monarch why he had failed. In October 1541 the explorer wrote to the king, saying he had done all he could to find the golden cities. Not only were there no cities of Cibola, nor any appreciable amounts of gold, Coronado said, there was very little in the way of metals of any kind in the lands he had explored. Instead, there were only scattered, poverty-stricken villages with houses made of sticks and animals skins. Fortunately for Coronado, Charles did not punish him for not finding the lost cities.

Although the Seven Cities of Cibola had yet to be found, these were not the only legendary cities Europeans had heard of. Shortly before Coronado set out into the future southwestern United States, another Spanish conquistador, Francisco Pizarro, entered what is now Peru, in South America's northwestern sector. There he and other Spaniards conquered the native dwellers, known as the Inca.

While this bloody episode unfolded, the Spaniards heard some of the local Indians talking about a formidable ruler who had a large realm located somewhere in the heart of the continent. According to the story, this great king was so rich that he covered his skin with gold dust. The sixteenth-century Spanish chronicler Gonzalo Fernández de Oviedo wrote that the fabled Indian leader "constantly goes about covered with gold ground [into dust] and as fine as ground salt. For it is his opinion that to wear any other adornment is less beautifying. . . . I would rather have the sweepings from the chamber of this monarch than that of the great melting establishments that have been set up for [the refining of gold] in Peru."[7]

Because of this legend, the Spaniards called the wealthy native king El Dorado, meaning "the gilded one." (*Gilded* means "gold covered.") Soon they started referring to his kingdom and capital city as El Dorado as well. Various native stories suggested the city might lie near Lake Guatavita, not far from modern Bogotá, Colombia.

Pizarro's half-brother, Gonzalo, became so smitten by the legend of El Dorado that he decided to try to find it. He also set his sights on finding another fabled lost city and kingdom known as La Canela, or "the Land of Cinnamon." Because cinnamon was an extremely popular delicacy in Europe, coming into possession of large numbers of cinnamon trees would make someone rich. But just as Coronado had failed

The mythical gold-covered king El Dorado, center, is depicted in this engraving. Neither El Dorado the king nor the fabled lost city were ever found.

to locate the Seven Cities, Gonzalo Pizarro never found either El Dorado or La Canela. Later, in the early 1600s, English explorer and adventurer Walter Raleigh also searched for El Dorado but could not find it. These supposedly real and wealthy lost cities remained elusive and later proved to be mere myths.

Searching for Aztlán

Nevertheless, in the years that followed, hopeful Spanish and other European individuals who could afford to do so continued to search for lost cities in the Americas, including what is now the United States. Meanwhile, Britain established its thirteen American colonies on North America's eastern seaboard. By the mid-1700s these colonies were highly prosperous and had developed a growing reading public. Stories about El Dorado circulated, some claiming it lay in the vast lands lying west of the British colonies. Also popular then, and in the early years of the infant United States, were tales of other lost cities, as pointed out by American historian Henry J. Sage: "[Such] myths about [legendary cities in] America developed early. Books were written about Utopias [ideal societies] in the West. Myths of cities of gold and silver ('El Dorado') flourished. Early settlers and investment company hustlers tried to make the colonies sound as attractive as possible to attract colonists."[8]

Thus, a major reason stories about lost cities were common in colonial America and the early United States was that a few enterprising people saw the potential for big profits. Clearly, people were fascinated by such tales. Furthermore, books on that subject could be counted on to sell well, a situation that still exists today in U.S. literary markets.

Partly for that reason, over time, speculation about lost cities in North America increasingly fell to historians, both professional and amateur, and to less-educated writers trying to make a name for themselves. In the 1800s and early 1900s, several individuals wrote books in which they laid

Aztlán Becomes a Modern Symbol

The mythical city or kingdom of Aztlán later became a symbol for a number of Mexican nationalist groups. In the 1960s, for instance, activist Oscar Zeta Acosta led a Mexican group that wanted the United States to give back the lands it had won in the Mexican-American War. Acosta called these lands Aztlán.

out their theories about such cities. Sometimes the evidence they presented was sound, while other times it was based on hearsay and/or faulty scholarship. Either way, their writings served to promote new myths about legendary cities, stories that continued to capture the attention of some segments of the U.S. reading public.

One such story involved Aztlán, the mythical original home of the Aztec people. The myth came directly out of actual Aztec folklore. The Aztec claimed that before they settled in southern Mexico and established a mighty empire there, they had migrated from a place far to the north. This fabulous city and country, called Aztlán, the story went, was the homeland of the Nahua people, who spoke a language called Nahuatl. Some of the original Nahua stayed in Aztlán. Others, including the Aztecs, who called themselves the Mexica, left in the year 1064 and journeyed southward. (The Mexica themselves never used the term *Aztec*, which was coined much later by European scholars.)

Many of the initial American historians who wrote about Aztlán said that, if it was indeed a real city, it was likely located somewhere in northern Mexico. However, over time, a growing number of experts came to believe it lay north of the Colorado River, in Texas or farther west, in Colorado or Utah. Archaeologist Kelley Hays-Gilpin of Northern Arizona University has proposed that the people who would one day become the Mexica/Aztec initially lived in Mexico. About five thousand years ago, she says, they migrated northward and settled in Utah. There they established Aztlán and prospered for many centuries. Finally, a few hundred years before the Spanish arrived in Mexico, the tribe migrated back into the Valley of Mexico, subjugated the local Indians, and built an impressive empire. In this scenario the legendary city of Aztlán was situated somewhere in the future United States.

Atlantean Colonies in America?

If the mythical Aztlán *was* in Utah or elsewhere in the American West, its exact location remains unknown. The same can be said for some other lost cities believed by some to

have existed in the United States—the American colonies of Atlantis. Lost Atlantis—seen variously as an island, continent, and city—was first mentioned by the ancient Greek thinker Plato. He claimed that it lay beyond the Pillars of Heracles (the Strait of Gibraltar), in the Atlantic Ocean; hence its name, Atlantis.

Over the centuries, especially in the early modern era, writers suggested a wide variety of locations for Atlantis. These ranged from North Africa to Scandinavia and from Brazil to the Caribbean islands. But the most popular site remained the Atlantic Ocean, where supposedly Atlantis thrived until a terrible disaster caused it to sink beneath the waves.

This myth continued to fascinate people around the world well into the 1800s. One of them was a small-time politician, lawyer, and amateur historical researcher named Ignatius Donnelly. Latching onto the topic to the point of obsession, he accumulated research for years and in 1882

This map depicts the Aztec migration from Aztlán to Tenochtitlán between the ninth and thirteenth centuries. Such evidence led the Spanish to believe that Aztlán still existed.

Was America Itself Atlantis?

For more than three centuries, a number of well-known European and, later, American scholars suggested that the famous lost city and continent of Atlantis was actually North America, including what is now the United States. In 1583 Spanish historian Francisco de Gomara published his *History of the Indies*, in which he stated that America and Atlantis were one and the same. Later, in 1591, French astronomer and college professor Guillaume de Postel reached the same conclusion. He pointed out the odd similarity between the word *Atlantis* and the name of the Aztecs' mythical home to the north of Mexico—Aztlán. This clue, he proposed, showed that there was a strong possibility that North America was indeed Atlantis. Almost a century later, in 1689, French geographers Nicholas and Guillaume Sauson concluded that Gomara and Postel had been right. They published an atlas that indicated specific places in North America where various kings of Atlantis might have erected their capital cities. Even as late as the twentieth century, Scottish scholar Lewis Spence, who believed that Atlantis was a real place, carefully reviewed the evidence for the North America–Atlantis link, although he expressed doubts that it was true.

published a large volume titled *Atlantis: The Antediluvian World*. (*Antediluvian* means "before the flood," a reference to Noah's Flood in the Judeo-Christian Bible.) It received rave reviews. The *St. Paul Dispatch* called it "one of the notable books of the decade, nay, of the century,"[9] and the *New York Star* called Donnelly "the most unique figure in our national history."[10] In addition, the volume became a best seller in the United States, and demand for it was also high in Europe and elsewhere in the world.

Donnelly's central thesis was that human civilization first arose in Atlantis and then spread outward to other continents. Atlantean colonies appeared in Egypt, Greece, and other parts of the Old World, and similar colonies flourished in North America, including what later became the United States. He pointed to the towns of the so-called Mound Builders, Native Americans who erected large pyramid-like mounds in the eastern and central United States. These, he claimed, were the later, less technically advanced remnants of the Atlantean American cities. In his book Donnelly listed some of his "proof" for the connection between the Mound Builders and Atlantis, saying in part:

1. Their race [is similar to] the nations of Central America who possessed [Noah's] Flood legends, and whose traditions all point to an eastern, over-sea origin; while the many evidences of their race identity with the ancient Peruvians indicate that they were part of one great movement of the human race, extending from the Andes to Lake Superior, and, as I believe, from Atlantis to India.
2. The similarity of their civilization, and their works of stone and bronze, with the civilization of the Bronze Age in Europe.
3. The presence of great truncated mounds, kindred to the pyramids of Central America, Mexico, Egypt, and India. . . .
5. The fact that the settlements of the Mound Builders were confined to the valley of the Mississippi, and were apparently densest at those points where a population advancing up that stream [from Atlantis] would first reach high, healthy, and fertile lands.[11]

Faulty Evidence and Wrong Conclusions

Serious scientists and other scholars dismissed these weak, unsupported arguments out of hand. Over time they explained why nearly all of Donnelly's so-called evidence was faulty and his conclusions wrong. Most important of all, twentieth-century studies of the Atlantic seabed showed beyond a doubt that there had never been a large landmass in that waterway. So if Atlantis had once existed, it had not rested in the Atlantic.

In spite of these realities, however, Donnelly continued to enjoy support among Americans of all walks of life. As his book went through one new printing after another, he single-handedly created a myth that refused to go away. Large numbers of Americans passed the myth on to their children, who in turn did the same. As a result, new editions of Donnelly's book still appear every few years, and his idea that colonies of Atlantis once existed in the United States remains a strong possibility in some people's minds.

Aware that Donnelly's book is still popular today, the authors of *Bad Archaeology*, an online study that exposes and debunks scientific theories based on poor scholarship, tackled it. They state, "It is no exaggeration to say that this book (on its own) was responsible for the late nineteenth-century growth of interest in the lost continent and its subsequent popularity." They concede that "it is a remarkable book, showing a huge breadth of knowledge acquired through years of reading and research in the Library of Congress." Yet, they add, "The evidence amassed by Donnelly for an historical Atlantis is ultimately weak and has never commanded any serious academic support. Donnelly's *breadth* of knowledge may have been huge, but he lacked the *depth* of knowledge that would have allowed him to exercise his lawyer's critical faculties more effectively."[12]

One thing that Donnelly did prove quite effectively was that myths of legendary cities and lost civilizations remain as compelling today as they were in prior ages. Some experts claim that such tales may be especially popular in the United States and other places in the Americas. This is because large-scale cities have existed there for only a few centuries. It is common knowledge that, by contrast, Europe, Asia, and Africa had cities with public buildings, writing systems, and laws in very ancient times. Perhaps a bit jealously, therefore, some Americans are eager and quick to believe that

Donnelly's Heir

Scottish scholar Lewis Spence (1874–1955) was fascinated by Atlantis. He carried on the Atlantis-related research of Ignatius Donnelly, publishing many books, including *The Problem of Atlantis* (1924), *Atlantis in America* (1925), and *History of Atlantis* (1927).

wondrous legendary cities might also have existed in the dim past in their own homeland.

In fact, this may partially explain the continued popularity of Donnelly's scientifically disproved theory. It contends that Atlantis founded colonies in America that were equal in splendor and worth to those it established in Europe and Africa. Some Americans seem to interpret this to mean that Europe has little to teach America. It is an independent, somewhat defiant attitude that has been strongly held by many Americans since well before the colonies broke away from Britain in 1776. A Frenchman who visited the United States in 1831 agreed that the country was more than Europe's equal and remarked, with no small amount of awe, that America "exhibits in her social state an extraordinary phenomenon. Men are there seen on a greater [level of] equality in point of fortune and intellect . . . than in any other country of [Europe or] the world, or in any age of which history has preserved the remembrance."[13]

CHAPTER 2

Monsters on the Loose

During the United States' relatively short history of fewer than three centuries (compared to dozens of centuries for some European and Asian nations), it has accumulated or produced untold numbers of monsters. Some of these weird creatures were described in written literature. Others appeared in artwork, music, and films. Still others were introduced in the realm of folklore and myths, tales passed on at first orally and later in writing and visual representations.

The American monsters have been of numerous different kinds, shapes, and sizes. Historian W. Scott Poole writes:

> Americans have an undeniable taste for the monstrous in all its forms, a taste in evidence from the time of the earliest colonial settlements. The narrative of American history can be used as a tale of monsters slain and monsters beloved. Witches and other night creatures infested the New England woods, and . . . sea serpents trawled the waters of the [nearby] oceans. . . . Wild men and savage beasts prowled the virgin woodlands where America cut its railroads and canals [and] built its settlements.[14]

Legendary Sea Creatures

The sea monsters that "trawled the waters," in Poole's words, were among the more common, as well as more frightening, monsters sighted in the country's early years. Colonial sailors living and working along America's Atlantic coast claimed they saw mermaids, mermen (male versions of mermaids), sirens (mermaids who lured sailors by singing lovely songs), and all sorts of serpents. Folktales about such creatures spread far and wide.

Of these marine myths, perhaps the most famous was that of the terrifying sea serpent of 1817. In August of that year, a number of people claimed they saw it in the harbor at Gloucester, north of Massachusetts's capital of Boston. A few weeks later other sightings of it occurred along the shore of Long Island, in southern New York. One witness, Gloucester resident Matthew Gaffney, described its appearance and his close encounter with it, saying:

> I was in a boat, and was within 30 feet of him. His head appeared full as large as a four-gallon keg, his body as large [around] as a barrel, and his length that I saw I should judge 40 feet at least. The top of his head was of a dark color and the under-part of his head appeared nearly white, as did also several feet of his belly that I saw. . . . I have seen the animal at several other times, but never had as good a view of him as on this day.[15]

Members of Boston's Linnean Society, a local organization of scientists, investigated the sightings and interviewed Gaffney and other witnesses. One question they asked was how the beast moved through the water. Myth collector B.A. Botkin sums up the answers this way: "It was seen . . . sometimes in rapid motion, sometimes at rest. When moving, it appeared to curve its back in vertical undulations [ripples]. When at rest, its back seemed, at times, to be undulating, and others smooth. . . . It appeared to take little notice of surrounding objects [and] was not heard to utter any sounds."[16]

Large numbers of New England folk told and retold the story of the great serpent of 1817 in the years that followed. They also enjoyed hearing the repeated tale of a no less strange and scary sea creature. Called the giant kraken, it was supposedly some sort of huge, octopus-like beast. The general consensus among ordinary people with no scientific background was that it was a leftover from the prehistoric age when enormous creatures had roamed the seas. American folklore specialist Virginia Haviland offers a description of the creature: "In shape, he vaguely resembles a crab, with a hard, armored shell . . . over the mass of his body. This shell is of a mottled dark green, which blends with the dark green

An artist's rendering of the sea serpent that reportedly made several appearances in the harbor of Gloucester, Massachusetts, in 1817.

Investigating the Great Serpent

In the wake of claimed sightings of a sea serpent in Gloucester, Massachusetts, in 1817, Boston's Linnean Society sent a committee of experts to investigate. The group's preliminary statement said that the researchers had gathered "for the purpose of collecting any evidence which may exist respecting a remarkable animal, [called] a sea serpent."

The preliminary statement went on to explain the investigators' method, which was scientifically based in an attempt to eliminate fraud and mistaken conclusions and get at the truth. To this end, the witnesses were requested to answer several fact-finding questions, including:

When did you first see this animal? How often and how long at a time? At what times of the day? At what distance? . . . What was its general appearance? . . . How fast did it move and in what direction? . . . What were the size and shape of its head, and had the head ears, horns, or other appendages? . . . Had it gills or breathing holes, and where? Had it fins or legs, and where? . . . Did it utter any sound?

Quoted in B.A. Botkin, ed. *A Treasury of New England Folklore*. New York: Bonanza, 1988, p. 195.

of sea water. . . . His great tentacles, like giant lobster claws, extend from the side of the shell. He is not a pretty beast."[17]

Sometimes the kraken was sighted by sailors, who beat a hasty retreat from it. Other tales about the beast claimed it was finally killed by a huge, incredibly strong sailor named Alfred Stormalong, known as "Stormy" for short. Legends claimed that he boarded a special, overlarge ship built for him, the *Tuscarora*. Then he hunted down the kraken and nailed it with a colossal harpoon made of the hardest steel then known.

The stories about the kraken, giant serpents, and other strange sea creatures no doubt originated in part from two facts about America's eastern seaboard. First, that region, especially the northeastern part, had a long seafaring tradition. Second, sailors everywhere have always loved inventing, telling, and listening to tall tales, and American sailors were no exception. It is also possible that some of the stories of legendary sea monsters were based on sightings of real animals that were mistakenly identified.

Birth of a Monster

In contrast, the origins of another frightening mythical American monster are not so easy to explain away. Called the Jersey Devil, it was said to roam the Pine Barrens, a large, forested area lying not far north of Atlantic City, New Jersey. The creature was also sometimes known as the Leeds Devil. This was because its mother was supposedly Jane Leeds, wife of Daniel Leeds, an Englishman who arrived in the area in 1678 and gained ownership of a large portion of the Pine Barrens.

In the early 1700s, the story went, Jane, who was rumored to dabble in witchcraft, became pregnant with her thirteenth child. Thirteen is widely viewed as an unlucky number; it was certainly unlucky for the Leeds family, for when the child was born, it turned out to be horribly monstrous rather than human. Modern myth teller S.E. Schlosser describes the awful birth, saying:

> A storm was raging that night . . . when Mother Leeds was brought to bed in childbirth. The room was full of woman folk gathered to help her, more out of curiosity than good will. They had all heard the rumors that Mother Leeds was involved in witchcraft . . . [so] tension mounted when at last the baby arrived. [At first, it seemed] normal. But a few moments later, before their terrified eyes, the child began to change. The room erupted with screams as the child grew at an enormous rate, becoming taller than a man and changing into a beast which resembled a dragon, with a head like a horse, a snake-like body, and bat's wings. . . . With a harsh cry, it flew through the chimney and vanished into the storm.[18]

Many more sightings of the Jersey Devil occurred over the years. Some witnesses said it ate fish from streams and attacked cows, sometimes drying up their milk simply by breathing on them. The beast was also reported to devour small animals like cats and birds, and human children as well.

One of the more exciting incidents involving the monster took place in the year 1800. The renowned American naval hero Commodore Stephen Decatur needed some new cannonballs for his ship's big guns. So he went to an iron foundry that had recently been erected near the shore of the Pine Barrens. Decatur was standing in the foundry's firing range when he said he saw something odd fly by. It was as large as a man and hideously misshapen. Grabbing his musket, the commodore fired at the creature, but he was unsure of whether or not he actually hit it.

The Myth Grows

Among the later encounters with the monster was one involving another reputable witness, Joseph Bonaparte, the brother of France's famous military figure Napoléon Bonaparte. He lived in New Jersey off and on beginning in 1816. Joseph said he was sure he had glimpsed the infamous beast while on a hunting trip in the Pine Barrens.

Similar sightings in 1909 further increased the monster's fame and the frequency of written tellings of the still-expanding myth. So many residents of New Jersey said they saw either the creature or its footprints that year that a number of local authorities resorted to drastic measures. Fearing the monster would snatch children, some towns temporarily closed down their schools.

Later still, one night in 1927 a cab driver was on his way to Salem, New Jersey. When a tire went flat, he stopped to fix it, and suddenly, he recalled, the vehicle began vibrating to and fro. Glancing upward, the cabby spotted what looked like a big, winged man smashing its fists against cab's roof. The terrified cab driver wasted no time. He ran for his life and did not stop until he had reached the Salem police station, where he told his fantastic story.

The myth of the Jersey Devil did not die away after the 1927 incident. As recently as 1993, a New Jersey forest ranger claimed he was driving near the Pine Barrens and found the road up ahead blocked by a repulsive beast. It stood on its hind legs and had horns and black fur, he said. Fortunately, instead of attacking the ranger, it flew away.

To many New Jersey citizens, the stories about the Jersey Devil are simply part of a quaint, enduring myth. It has

The Jersey Devil

The Jersey Devil is said to have haunted the Pine Barrens of New Jersey for over 250 years.

been perpetuated over the years partly for fun, they say, and maybe sometimes to help attract tourists to the region in hopes of pumping up local businesses. In contrast, other skeptics suggest the monster was invented by the early residents of the Pine Barrens. According to this view, they enjoyed their privacy. So they created the creature in order to frighten outsiders and keep them out of the area.

Other modern observers of the Jersey Devil are not so sure of these explanations, however. One of them asks:

> If it was merely a myth then how do we explain the sightings of the creature and the witness accounts from reliable persons like businessmen, police officers, and even public officials? They are not easy to dismiss as hearsay or the result of heavy drinking. Could the Jersey Devil have been real after all? And if so, is it still out there in the remote regions of the Pine Barrens, just waiting to be found?[19]

Fooling the Hairy Man

The suggestion that the Jersey Devil was made up to frighten people away from the Pine Barrens may or may not be true. More certain is that American folklore is full of monsters purposely invented with the sole intention of scaring someone. Many of those made-up monsters fall under the general heading of or resemble a creature most often called the Bogeyman (or Bogieman or Boogieman).

One artist's rendering of the Bogeyman, which takes many forms depending on the tale.

Similar monsters existed in the folklore of Europe, Africa, and Asia and were carried to the Americas by immigrants from those places.

However, in colonial America and the early United States, these tales took on a peculiarly American character. Almost always, images of the American Bogeyman were employed by adults in order to frighten children into acting or not acting in certain ways. Typical were warnings such as, "If you're not a good boy the Bogeyman will get you!"

Moreover, in the backwoods regions of Appalachia and the South, elaborate tales about the monster developed beginning in the 1700s. Some of these were still circulating in the early twentieth century. One of the most often-told myths was that of the Hairy Man. As in some European and Asian versions, he was said to carry a sack in which to put a child or other victim. Supposedly, the creature carried the sack home, removed the victim, and ate him or her. The Hairy Man was also credited with having the power to turn himself into the likeness of any animal.

One day, the tale went, a little boy went down into a swamp to cut down some small trees to use in building a henhouse. His mother had warned him to be careful because the Hairy Man was said to lurk in the swamp sometimes. The boy figured that his mother was just repeating an old fairy tale, and he was not afraid. But that changed when, while chopping at a tree with his ax, he saw the Hairy Man sitting in a larger tree nearby. The creature, who had eyes like burning coals and big teeth with drool dripping from them, was smiling and staring right at the boy. Also, just like in the stories the boy's mother had told, the monster was clutching a big, empty sack.

The boy thought he might reason with the Hairy Man and convince him to go away and leave him alone. But the creature just laughed and said he intended to put the boy in his sack and take him to his lair. There the child would make him a tasty supper.

Seeing that he had no other choice, the boy decided to try a trick he had heard his mother mention. She said that if someone was able to fool the Hairy Man into doing something stupid, the monster would thereafter be forced to leave that person alone. So the boy challenged the Hairy Man to turn himself into a giraffe. To prove he could do it, the creature suddenly transformed himself into a giraffe with a tall, tall neck.

Then the boy said he doubted the Hairy Man could also turn himself into a pig. Again, the monster took the dare. His body twisted and shrunk from the form of a towering giraffe into that of a fat little pig. At that moment, the boy put his plan in motion. He jumped forward, scooped up the pig, slipped it into the Hairy Man's sack, and threw the sack into the river. The hairy Man was able to transform into a fish and swim away to safety. But because he had been badly fooled, from that day forward he had to leave the little boy alone.

Other Hairy Monsters

American mythology has long featured other hairy monsters besides the Hairy Man. Among them is Sasquatch, a shaggy, manlike creature said to inhabit deep forests. Others are werewolves, humans who supposedly sometimes turn into wolflike beasts and attack and eat people.

Stories about both of these monsters were common in the Old World, including both Europe and Asia. The inhabitants of the high mountains of northern India, Tibet, and southern China still abound in tales of giant, hairy, apelike creatures who dwell in remote forests and caves. Perhaps the most famous is the Yeti of Nepal and Tibet. Other names for the creature include Migoi, or "wild man," and Kang Admi, meaning "snow man." Meanwhile, stories about werewolves were told in Europe and Africa all through ancient and medieval times.

People from those lands brought such myths with them when they settled in colonial America. At the same time, several of the Indian tribes they encountered in America had their own legends of large hairy "men" who lived in deep forests, and stories of werewolves, too. Both the settlers and Native Americans continued to tell tales of such creatures living on the fringes of the wilderness for several generations.

Sasquatch's Myth Based on Fact?

Most scientists and other scholars think that the myth of Sasquatch has no scientific basis. However, a large minority of Americans are convinced that some unknown, apelike animal exists in the United States and has given rise to the myth. The strongest single piece of evidence the believers cite is the so-called Patterson-Gimlin film, which shows such a creature walking in a forest clearing. A researcher for the Animal Planet describes the film and its significance:

> The footage was obtained in a remote mountainous area in northern California in 1967. The two men involved were Roger Patterson and Bob Gimlin. Patterson was a rodeo rider from Yakima, Washington . . . [who] went down to northern California with a rented 16mm movie camera after hearing about numerous tracks in the valley around Bluff Creek. The footage has been repeatedly analyzed by scientists over the last 40 years. It has never been proven to be a hoax, yet various individuals have "confessed" to being the man in the costume over the years. All of the confessions contradict each other, and are strongly suspected of being hoaxes themselves.

Animal Planet. "Finding Bigfoot: The Evidence for Bigfoot." http://animal.discovery.com/tv/finding-bigfoot/bigfoot -evidence/index-03.html.

A still photograph of a sasquatch from the famed 1967 Patterson-Gimlin film.

Werewolves

Typical were the tales of werewolves in and around colonial Detroit, when it was still a French outpost in the Michigan wilderness. In one story a man approached a local witch and with her help sold his soul to the devil. With the latter's help, she cast a spell on the man that made him change at will into what the French called a loup-garou, or werewolf. One day,

The French myth of the loup-garou, or werewolf, resurfaced in the Michigan wilderness in the 1800s.

according to this myth, he transformed into that bloodthirsty creature and lunged at a young woman. But because she was praying before an image of the Virgin Mary at the time, a shell of goodness protected her, and the loup-garou suddenly turned to stone.

In another werewolf legend from that region, a wolf-man snatched a bride from the midst of her wedding ceremony. The anguished groom searched for years and eventually caught up to the monster, as told by noted American folklorist Charles M. Skinner:

> The lover finally came upon the creature and chased it to the shore [of Lake Michigan], where its footprint is still seen in one of the boulders. But the [werewolf] leaped into the water and disappeared. In his crazy fancy, the lover declared that it had jumped down the throat of a catfish, and that is why the [people of that region] have a prejudice against catfish as an article of diet.[20]

The Bigfoot Hoaxers

Sasquatch/Bigfoot may yet prove to be a real creature. But much of the evidence for it has been created by deliberate hoaxers. Many people have admitted to making fake Bigfoot footprints. One was Rant Mullens, who in 1982 revealed he had been doing it since 1930.

Sasquatch and Bigfoot

The locations of the monsters in such myths changed over time. As people cut down the forests of the eastern sectors of America and in their place built networks of cities and roads, tales of hairy man-like monsters became confined mainly to the American West. Sasquatch, who increasingly came to be called "Bigfoot" as well, became the central character in these stories.

In the twentieth century a number of people theorized that the creature was not a monster in the traditional sense—that is, a terrible, evil, supernatural, or depraved being. Rather, they said, it might be part of a small community of prehistoric humans that survived down to the present by hiding in densely forested areas. If that was the case, the myth was based on a real living thing.

A huge Bigfoot carving greets tourists outside of the Willow Creek–China Flat Museum in Northern California. The museum is home to a large Bigfoot exhibit.

Most scientists remain skeptical, however. As scientific investigator Ben Radford explains:

> Ultimately, the biggest problem with the argument for the existence of Bigfoot is that no bones or bodies have been discovered. . . . If the Bigfoot creatures [in] the United States are really out there, then each passing day should be one day closer to their discovery. [It's

hard] to believe that thousands of giant, hairy, mysterious creatures are constantly eluding capture and discovery and have for a century or more. At some point, a Bigfoot . . . must wander onto a freeway and get killed by a car, or get shot by a hunter, or die of natural causes and be discovered by a hiker. Each passing . . . year and decade that go by without definite proof of the existence of Bigfoot make its existence less and less likely. On the other hand, if Bigfoot is instead a self-perpetuating [myth] with no genuine creature at its core, the stories, sightings, and legends will likely continue unabated for centuries.[21]

Our Darker Side

Sea monsters, the Jersey Devil, various versions of the Bogeyman, werewolves, and Sasquatch/Bigfoot are only a few among the multitudes of monsters that have prowled the corridors of American mythology. Some of the others include a ruthless rider, the Headless Horseman; a frightening flyer called Mothman; and the Red Dwarf, an ill-behaved imp said to dwell in dark places beneath Detroit.

It is only natural to ask why it is that Americans have filled their folklore with so many dreadful, although often colorful, monsters. According to Poole, one reason is that deeply embedded in the culture lie disturbed feelings that make people both believe in and envision monsters. As a result, people create folktales and myths about such creatures on a regular basis. "Monsters are not just fears of the individual psyche [inner mind]," Poole says, "but are concoctions of the public imagination, reactions to cultural influences, social change, and historical events."[22] Entire segments of human communities can feel collective guilt for bad or unfortunate actions or events from that community's past, he explains. Such subconscious agitation or worries can

The Headless Horseman

The rider on horseback who lacked a head was long one of the scariest American mythical monsters. American writer Washington Irving made it famous in his 1820 short story "The Legend of Sleepy Hollow," but the character originated in Celtic and German myths of medieval times.

The Mystery of Mothman

Brian Dunning, producer of *Skeptoid*, a weekly radio and online scientific analysis of weird phenomena, here sums up one of the more famous American monster myths—that of the creature known as Mothman.

> The gravediggers were the first to see the strange being. It rose from the tree like a giant bird taking flight, but as it soared overhead, it began to look more like an angel, a man with wings. But it was dark and brown, more grotesque than radiant, more like a demon than an angel. The news spread.

> He was seen again three nights later, when two young couples saw his red glowing eyes in the trees by the side of the road late at night. . . .

> [In] November of 1966 in the vicinity of Point Pleasant in the low country of West Virginia . . . the demon was seen at least four more times, either as a tall dark man prowling outside houses with his red eyes or flying overhead on leathery wings. . . .

> In December of 1967, a little more than a year after the Mothman made headlines, the 40-year-old Silver Bridge connecting Point Pleasant with Gallipolis, Ohio . . . collapsed under the weight of rush hour traffic. 46 people died. . . .

> Why, more than 40 years later, do we still remember the Mothman? . . . Why is he considered a harbinger of disasters? He didn't hurt anybody . . . yet [some people] believe that when he appears, bridges collapse and people die, even though there [is no definite proof for it].

Brian Dunning. "The Mothman Cometh." *Skeptoid*, June 23, 2009. http://skeptoid.com/episodes/4159.

cause some people to interpret natural or harmless phenomena as dangerous and/or monstrous things.

Middlebury College sociology professor Laurie Essig delves even deeper into the American psyche to look for reasons for the American fascination for strange or threatening monsters. She says that belief in them brings with it the basic assumption that someone else, not oneself, is the monster. Such belief "allow[s] us to cleanse ourselves of all that we fear. . . . By projecting monstrosity onto others, we can imagine it doesn't reside in us. By laughing at or even hating the freaks on stage [at a carnival], we can ignore the monstrosity of our own [mistakes, prejudices, and poor choices]."[23]

In a very real way, therefore, mythical monsters are, as Poole puts it, "living representations of our [darker side],"[24] a part of us that extends back to the very emergence of humans from their animal past. "Indeed," says Poole, "almost all of the monster forms that delight and terrify modern America [can be traced] back to the origins of human society,"[25] when in a sense *we* were the monsters.

CHAPTER 3

Ghosts Haunt the Living

Myths about ghosts are universal, having existed in all cultures throughout history. Such tales have usually been intertwined in various ways with the realms of religion and superstition. For instance, most religious faiths advocate that ghosts are the spirits of deceased people. Meanwhile, superstition, the irrational belief that something assumed by most people to be unreal is in fact real, often causes some people, religious or not, to claim they believe in ghosts.

The earliest American myths about ghosts appeared in the Puritan colonies of Massachusetts, in New England, in the early to mid-1600s. The Puritans were fundamentalist Christians who strongly believed in the existence of evil, which they saw as a traditional opponent of God, his angels, and other forces of good. The devil, demons, witches, and ghosts, which they more often called phantoms, were all manifestations of evil in Puritan eyes and lore.

Society in early New England recognized several different motives or reasons why ghosts might interact with the living. One example was "the accusing ghost who returns to avenge a wrong," B.A. Botkin points out. There were also phantoms that were called forth to do mischief by witches or leaders of evil cults. Still another kind of early New England ghost,

Botkin says, was "the devil-doomed spirit condemned [by God] to the endless repetition of a [difficult menial] task."[26]

It did not take long for other early American colonies to develop numerous ghost myths of their own. "Every town and hamlet had their favorite (or their dreaded) spirit," folklorist Kemp P. Battle explains. "The place where a person drowned or the house in which someone died was soon caught in a gathering mist of rumor. All it took was one reliable witness, swearing total sobriety, to say he saw someone known to be already dead and buried, and a ghost [myth] was born."[27]

Many of these tales passed along to later generations of Americans as part of the country's growing collection of folklore. Over time, as scientific principles and studies were increasingly accepted in society, the incidence of belief in the ghosts described in those myths decreased. Yet even today a surprisingly large number of people still hold those beliefs. A 2011 Gallup/Associated Press poll found that 34 percent of Americans absolutely think that ghosts are real. Moreover, another 22 percent say they might be real, and if they *are*, they are most likely the spirits of dead people. Considering these relatively high figures, it is no wonder that ghost stories remain such an enduring and popular part of American mythology.

Phantom Curses

Not only have large numbers of Americans long enjoyed reading or listening to ghost stories, over time they categorized these tales into general types of ghost myths. For example, tales of haunted houses, in which ghosts reside in specific homes for many years, are both common and popular. But no less trendy and widely told are stories about ghost ships (vessels inhabited only by ghosts), the survival of the mean-spirited ghosts of notorious pirates, and phantom curses (cases in which ghosts of humans or animals are sent by witches to plague living persons).

Myths of phantom curses were common in the Puritan colonies, probably because belief in witches and their evil powers were so widespread there. Typical was the tall tale

The earliest American myths about ghosts appeared in the Puritan colony of Massachusetts in the early 1600s.

of colonist John Kemble and the phantom puppies. Kemble was looking for a new dog and heard that a woman named Susanna Martin had a female dog who had recently had a new litter.

It turned out that Martin was a witch who did not like Kemble and wanted to cause him trouble. When Kemble was out walking one evening, he felt dizzy and increasingly had trouble staying on his feet. Then he saw what appeared to be a cute little puppy in the path up ahead. When he went to pet it, the animal started nipping at his legs. Eventually, the man became frightened and swung his ax at the puppy, at which point something weird happened. "The Thing leaped aside and vanished into the ground," one myth teller recalls. "Kemble stared about him, rubbed his eyes and stumbled on. Up the shadowy road waited another Thing, a large puppy, black as coal, and vicious. It sprang for his throat, his belly, and darting behind him made for his shoulders. Swinging his ax made no impression on it at all."[28]

In the myth, Kemble continued to be attacked by the so-called puppies. Finally realizing they were hounds from hell—evil ghosts in puppy-form—he invoked Jesus Christ's name, and they suddenly disappeared. It was thought that witches, demons, and other evil beings could not tolerate even the mention of God's or Jesus's name. This was only one example of the way early American ghost stories derived from and relied heavily on religious beliefs and imagery. Ghosts were the work of the devil and therefore opposed to God; similarly, only God could properly drive ghosts away.

Clearly, the myth of the phantom puppies came from a place and time in which such stories made some sort of moral or religious statement. The tale of Kemble's encounter with evil ghosts that looked like puppies reinforced the commonly held notion that witches, most often females, dwelled among honest, God-fearing citizens. These women were dangerous, and steadfast belief in God was the only way to ensure that He would intervene and save people from the evils that witches had unleashed on the community.

Ghost Ships

In contrast, ghost-ship myths, which became fashionable in the 1700s, had less to do with God and morality and more with the creation of spooky atmosphere. The main purpose of ghost-ship tales was to entertain, especially in communities on the seacoasts. Most people who heard such stories in dockyards, taverns, and homes in those areas were closely

Even the Educated Believed in Ghosts

Many uneducated and poor folk who lived in the early New England colonies believed in ghosts. But they were not alone. Even society's most educated individuals, including early colonial scientists like Puritan minister Cotton Mather, held that ghosts were real.

Captain Sandovate's Ghost Ship

One of the more familiar American ghost-ship myths involves a Spanish sea captain named Don Sandovate, who sailed to the New World in search of treasure. After he and his crew found a cache of gold and other valuables, the story goes, the crew mutinied and took Sandovate's hefty share of the loot. They tied him to the main mast and left him there to rot. Finally, he died of exposure and starvation, and the new captain was so mean-spirited he ordered that the body be left where it was. Eventually, an enormous storm blew up and carried the vessel far out into the Atlantic. There it sank, and all members of the crew perished. Not long after this occurred, people along North America's eastern coast began seeing a ghost ship that appeared near the shore shortly before bad weather set in. They claimed they saw the body of a well-dressed man tied to the main mast, as well as several skeletons arrayed in torn clothes. A few witnesses had heard about Sandovate's fate and suggested that his greedy, cruel crewmen were now paying for his foul murder by roaming the seas eternally, unable to find final resting places.

familiar with ships and maritime culture. So the idea of ships piloted by ghosts was particularly disquieting and frightening to them.

Also, in retrospect these tales were among the first examples of the popular genre of the horror story in American culture. That genre was highly popular in Europe in late medieval and early modern times, and European settlers who made new homes in what is now the Untied States carried on the tradition in their new communities. Likewise, that tradition survives today in the form of short stories, novels, TV shows, and movies designed to amuse audiences by scaring them. Battle writes that these myths have always been

> examples of mystery and the macabre [horrible] on the American landscape, and they are part of that

ongoing process of storytelling that modern yarn-spinners like Stephen King still exploit. After all, we have not changed [emotionally] at all [since colonial times]. We still don't understand the things that scare us, and stories of horror . . . stay with us long after the lights have been turned off.[29]

Perhaps the most famous ghost ship of all time was the *Flying Dutchman*. A Dutch ship, as its name suggests, it was said to have disappeared, but soon afterward it reappeared. After that it was condemned to wander through the seas as a ghost ship, unable to land in any port. Sightings of the vessel were recorded periodically by Americans up and down the eastern seaboard, and over the years the ship's legend inspired a number of American artists, poets, musicians, and novelists to depict it in their works.

Perhaps the most famous ghost ship is the Flying Dutchman, *depicted faintly in the background of this painting. The tale has inspired many American artists, poets, musicians, and novelists.*

There were American-built ghost ships, too. One of the most often-told tales of such vessels in colonial America was that of the "*Palatine* Light." In 1752, one version of the myth claimed, a large vessel called the *Palatine* departed a German port carrying numerous Europeans who desired to build new homes and lives in colonial America. When the ship was well out into the Atlantic Ocean, the captain suddenly died (or in another version was murdered). The crew then kept all the remaining food for themselves, allowing the passengers to starve.

Finally, the *Palatine*'s crew abandoned the passengers, who died, and the boat drifted away. After that, from time to time it was spotted by people living on America's coasts. "She was somehow changed into a ship of fire," one early modern storyteller wrote, "rising up from the waters of Block Island Sound," which lies along Rhode Island's southern coast. The mysterious ship was "manned by an invisible captain and crew," a sight that sent shivers up witnesses' spines. After its flaming light had caught the attention of onlookers on the shore, the vessel's "hull, spars, ropes, and sails all slowly vanished in the air or settled down into the deep,"[30] until the next time it rose up to terrify the living.

Blackbeard's Ghost

Another very common category of ghost myth in colonial America and the early United States was that of the creepy, frightening spirits of dead pirates. In modern American culture, pirates are usually cartoonlike characters like those portrayed in Walt Disney's Pirates of the Caribbean exhibit and the popular movies based on it. They are typically depicted as being quaint, humorous, and dressed in colorful costumes.

In early America, however, pirates were very real criminals. Greedy, mean, and murderous, they terrorized the islands of the Caribbean and the coasts of the southern colonies (and later states) of Florida, Georgia, South and North Carolina, and Virginia. According to a spokesperson for a modern maritime museum, "Stories about pirate brutality meant that many of the most famous pirates had a terrifying reputation, and they advertised this by flying various gruesome flags including the 'Jolly Roger' with its picture of skull and crossbones."[31]

Thus, most people were scared to death of pirates. So it is not surprising that they also viewed tales of the ghosts of pirates as no less frightening. Scariest of all was the myth of the ghost of Blackbeard, whose real name was Edward Teach. His attacks reached their peak in about 1718. In his notorious pirate vessel, called *Queen Anne's Revenge*, he terrorized people in ships and communities along the coasts of South Carolina and other nearby American colonies. Legend claims that his ghost still haunts those shores.

It was not the mere fact that Blackbeard was well-organized and adept at pirating that made him so terrifying to most people. He also "liked to psychologically defeat his victims before ever raising a sword or firing a shot," a noted researcher of ghosts and hauntings writes.

> While attacking other ships, he dressed in all black and wore long black ribbons in his braided beard. He stuffed pieces of rope under his hat and lit them so that they smoldered, billowing smoke around his head, giving him a scary unworldly like appearance to his victims. He always attacked at dawn or dusk with the sun behind his back so that the ships and crew he victimized would not see him coming until it was too late.[32]

The horrifying story of the emergence of Blackbeard's ghost began at the close of a long and bloody battle fought at Teach's Hole. This was the name Blackbeard coined for his hideout near Ocracoke Island, on North Carolina's coast. In the battle, a military officer sent by the governor of the Virginia Colony to end Blackbeard's reign of terror personally fought with and

Blackbeard's Ship Found?

Although not a traditional treasure composed of money and jewels, one of Blackbeard's most treasured possessions was unearthed in 1996. A team of researchers found what they believe to be the remains of the pirate's famous ship, the *Queen Anne's Revenge*, off the coast of North Carolina.

Edward Teach, better known as Blackbeard, had a fearsome appearance and spread terror along the Carolina coast in the early eighteenth century. Ghost stories about him began to appear after his violent death in 1720.

shot the pirate. But Blackbeard seemed unfazed and fought on. So the officer brutally slashed him with a sword. When this also failed to stop Blackbeard, his opponents had to shoot him five more times before he finally fell dead. To make sure he was fully dead, the officer beheaded him, tossed his body into the sea, and hung the head from a ship's mast. Incredibly, the legend says, the bodiless head continued to speak for some time, causing onlookers quite a fright.

According to the myth, that weird incident proved only the beginning of a new reign of terror for Blackbeard. In the years that followed, people along the North Carolina coast claimed they saw the pirate's headless body walking on local beaches or swimming in the nearby waters. Some said the grisly phantom appeared to be searching for his lost head. Others said the zombie-like body sometimes dug holes in the sand, suggesting it was looking for one of the treasure chests that Blackbeard was reported to have buried. In fact, the story claimed, the infamous pirate's ghost will neither rest nor go away until it or someone else finds his lost treasures.

Hoping for Easy Riches

Like tales about ghost ships, those about pirates' ghosts belonged to the growing American horror story genre. However, the pirate variety of ghost tale had a somewhat deeper cultural meaning as well. Like the story of Blackbeard's ghost, most of these myths depicted pirates burying one or more chests containing a fabulous treasure. The motive was to keep the treasure away from the authorities, as well as from rival pirates. Usually in these stories, the leading pirate ended up dying before digging the treasure back up. His ghost then haunted the region, intent on finding the treasure and/or scaring people away from the burial spot.

It must be remembered that most colonial Americans believed in the existence of ghosts as strongly as they feared pirates. Moreover, many of the pirate ghost tales depicted real pirates, like Blackbeard, rather than fictional ones. As a result, many people believed that the treasures mentioned in these stories were real, too. (In reality few real pirates buried their treasures.)

Based on these myths, some intrepid folk, in both that and later ages,

A Ghost from the Past

Blackbeard's famous phantom was the subject of the 1968 comic movie *Blackbeard's Ghost,* starring the great British actor Peter Ustinov. It depicts the pirate's spirit moving forward in time and humorously interacting with people in the present.

actually went out and searched for buried pirate chests in hopes of striking it rich. Almost none ever did. Yet the hope always remained. In addition to scaring people, therefore, these tales gave some people hope for quick, easy riches in the same way that state and national lotteries do today.

Although most of these purported pirate treasures were said to be buried in the ground, a few were not. In one famous pirate-ghost myth, for example, the pirate Black Bartelmy managed to take his treasure with him on his ship after he died. A real pirate, as Blackbeard was, Bartelmy was feared all along the Atlantic American coast during the early 1700s. Bartelmy periodically captured merchant ships and raided and pillaged towns and was said to be so cruel and pitiless that he murdered his own wife and children.

Also a very successful pirate, Bartelmy reportedly accumulated some five hundred chests of gold, silver, jewels, and other loot. He was so greedy that instead of sharing the treasure with his loyal crewmen, he had his first mate cut all their throats in their sleep. Then Bartelmy murdered the first mate. Soon afterward, however, the nasty buccaneer unwittingly stepped into a patch of quicksand and died. Supposedly, his evil ghost rose up from the quicksand, flew to his ship, and sailed it out into the Atlantic.

Many years later people along the Atlantic coast started having a strange experience. In one typical instance, a lighthouse keeper saw a flare shoot up into the sky. Thinking a ship might be in trouble, he sailed his lifeboat out into the choppy waves to attempt a rescue, but then came upon "an ancient galleon with tattered sails," in S.E. Schlosser's words. "Its decks were piled high with treasure chests spilling over with gold. Astride the deck was a solitary man in black. The evil pirate grinned wickedly . . . gesturing grandly with his cutlass. As the breakers overwhelmed [his] boat, the last thing the [lighthouse] keeper . . . heard was the sound of Black Bartelmy's ghost laughing."[33]

Over the years, some treasure hunters tried to locate the remains of Bartelmy's ship. They believed there was a chance

Treasure Rarely Buried

It is perhaps ironic that one of the central tenets of pirate ghost tales—the burial of a wealthy treasure—was actually a rare occurrence. As expert observer Teresa Coppens points out, "Although it is a romantic notion and the idea of finding buried treasure appeals to every person, pirates rarely buried treasure." She continues:

> Most loot gained during an attack was quickly divided up amongst the crew. They would rather spend it immediately than bury it. A lot of the treasure gained consisted of perishable items like fabric, silk,

and food. Pirates understood that their life was hard and they might be gone tomorrow, so they preferred to spend immediately rather than later. Only two instances of true buried treasure have been well documented. In [one that happened in] 1573, [English sea captain] Francis Drake attacked mule trains carrying Spanish silver from a South American mine to the Caribbean from where it would be transported to Europe. Drake amassed about 170,000 lbs of silver which was too much to transport back to his ship. The crew buried most of the treasure after loading as much as they could. The same night, English ships returned to the shore and recovered their buried treasure that Drake and his men had left behind.

Teresa Coppens. "Pirates: Separating Fact from Mythology." HubPages. http://teresacoppens.hubpages.com /hub/Pirates-Separating-Fact-from-Mythology.

Although many myths revolve around buried pirate treasure, pirates, in fact, rarely buried their loot.

Many people along the Atlantic Coast claimed to have seen a Spanish galleon, laden with treasure, with the ghost of Black Bartelmy on board.

it might contain an extremely valuable cargo. But to date, no one has been able to find the vessel and its legendary chests of booty.

Haunted Houses

Another category of American ghost myths—the haunted house—became common in the nineteenth century and especially popular in the twentieth century. The haunted houses of American myth are not the many staged haunted houses that suddenly appear near the Halloween season and use special effects, actors, and scenery to create their ghosts and frightening atmosphere.

Real haunted houses—that is, houses that are believed to contain real ghosts—are fewer in number. They also need no special effects. This is partly because the mere claim or thought that a house is haunted can make some people too scared to enter the premises, or at least uneasy. One visitor to a famous American haunted house remarked, "Personally, I felt a little ill at ease when passing the bedroom doorway that was opposite the top of the stairs. . . . I'm sure [the former owner's] spirit patrols that general area, so there's no telling you exactly where you might sense something."[34]

Just as tales about pirate ghosts are usually based on real pirates, myths about haunted houses are more often than not based on real houses. Indeed, every U.S. state lays claim to at least a few houses that figure prominently in well-known local myths. One of the oldest and most famous of the U.S. haunted houses is Ringwood Manor, in northeastern New Jersey. The mansion was built in 1740 and went through major renovations in 1807. A cemetery on the property contains the graves of several of the former owners and their family members.

The myth of the manor's assortment of ghosts claims that these apparitions are the spirits of former owners, house workers, and people who visited the property. Supposedly, they continue to haunt the house because they are distressed, unhappy, or otherwise upset over events either in their own lives or in the house's later history. Paranormal researcher Jill Stefko lists some of these ghosts:

> [A man] was decapitated in a mining accident near the estate's grounds. [It is] believed his ghost haunted an upstairs bedroom. [A former owner named] General Erskine is buried behind the manor's pond. Witnesses have seen him at dusk sitting on his grave looking across the water. There's [also] an unmarked grave filled with bodies of French soldiers who fought in

the Revolutionary War on the grounds. Their specters have been seen and heard speaking French. There's the phantom of a maid haunting a small second floor bedroom where she, allegedly, was beaten to death. People have heard crying, footsteps and objects dropping [coming] from the empty room.[35]

Although myths of encountering ghosts in haunted houses have been and continue to be used to entertain people, their primary cultural basis remains embedded in traditional religious beliefs. The fact is that the vast majority of Americans believe in life after death. They hold that the human soul survives the demise of the human body. Most souls go to heaven or hell, the general thinking goes, but a few linger

Haunted house myths abound across the United States. Myrtles Plantation, pictured, in Louisiana is known as one of the most haunted houses in the country.

on earth and sometimes interact, as ghosts, with the living.

In reality this scenario may or may not be true, but the fact is that many Americans believe it is true. Some experts suggest that this is in large part because they *want* it to be true. They badly want to believe that death does not mark the complete end of human existence. "We all find it much easier to believe in things that we want to be true," researcher Emma Barden says. "Psychologists call this the 'confirmation bias' and it is particularly acute at a time [when a loved one dies]. By believing in ghosts, we reassure ourselves that death isn't the end."[36] Thus, regardless of whether or not ghosts actually exist, myths about them remain popular partly because they reassure people that something they dearly want to be real *is* in fact real.

CHAPTER 4

Tall Tales About Heroes

Most of the classic myths of American heroes emerged from the legends and literary works of the frontier. Its heyday of fame and popularity was in the period lasting from the late 1700s to about 1900 and somewhat beyond. This was when pioneers from the eastern states trekked through, settled in, and built up what came to be known as the American West, which began in the Appalachian Mountains and moved farther and farther westward over time.

The West was a region in which both a real culture and a mythic society grew up. These were closely connected, as the area's unusual and often grandiose physical traits greatly contributed to its eventual mythic qualities. For example, the West was a vast, uncharted wilderness filled with natural wonders and lurking dangers. So it is not surprising that America's national frontier, or backwoods, heroes were as big, bold, brash, and tough as the land that spawned them. Myth teller B.A. Botkin colorfully defined the mythic West as "an American fairyland of strong men and giants who perform the impossible."[37] University of North Carolina researcher Diana Chike points out that these larger-than-life characters "can be viewed as a reflection of the exaggerated scale of a vast frontier and of the rugged pioneers that faced and overcame its challenges." She adds that the often witty and/or amusing tales describing such heroes were in part "a humorous means of coping with the hardships and violence encountered by the pioneers in their new land. [Those] tall tales have also been perceived as an attempt at creating a national identity for a very young country by constructing a 'history' through such folk heroes as Davy Crockett . . . John Henry, and Pecos Bill—American counterparts to the folk heroes of [Europe]."[38]

Some of these mythical heroes were characters based on real people. Davy Crockett, an actual backwoodsman who often told highly exaggerated stories about himself, was a prime example. Others were "spun from whole cloth," meaning made-up or fictional. Among their number were Pecos Bill, John Henry, and Paul Bunyan. As Botkin says, in each of these characters there was something of "a showman, with a flair for prodigious [remarkable] stories, jokes, and stunts, and a general capacity for putting himself over [explaining himself]. [An integral part of] the frontier or pioneer myth . . . the backwoodsman was the first of our tall men, whose words were tall talk and whose deeds were tall tales."[39]

A period illustration depicts frontiersman Davy Crockett killing a bear with only his knife. Many tall tales sprang up in American folklore about Crockett, who was not above embellishing his own accounts of his exploits.

Tallest of the Tall Men

The tallest of these authentically American tall men was the lumberjack to end all lumberjacks—Paul Bunyan, who legend claimed was born in Maine. Indeed, everything about him was big. It was said that when he was fewer than two weeks old, he already weighed more than 100 pounds (45kg) and that at the age of nine months he caused minor earthquakes just by rolling over! A popular modern folklorist lists some of his other early feats:

> As a newborn, Paul Bunyan could holler so loud he scared all the fish out of the rivers and streams. All the local frogs started wearing earmuffs so they wouldn't go deaf when Paul screamed for his breakfast. His parents had to milk two dozen cows morning and night to keep his milk bottle full and his mother had to feed him ten barrels of [oatmeal] every two hours to keep his stomach from rumbling and knocking the house down. . . . His parents were at their wits' end! They decided to build him a raft and floated it off the coast of Maine. When Paul turned over, it caused a 75-foot tidal wave.[40]

As an adult, Paul had a voice so big and loud that other lumberjacks who worked around him had to wear earmuffs. Also, his lungs were so strong that he called to other lumberjacks by whistling through a huge, hollowed-out tree trunk. One day, it was said, he blew through the thing too hard, and his excess breath knocked down a dozen acres of pine trees. Moreover, each time he sneezed, the gust of wind he created peeled the roof off the nearest house.

Also unusually big and strong was Paul's trusty companion, Babe the Blue Ox. Babe was so large, in fact, that seven ax handles could be placed end to end between his eyes. One story told how he could drag the logs cleared from 640 acres (259ha) of land at one time and

Statues of Paul and Babe

Paul Bunyan's myth became so popular in the American heartland that towns across the Midwest and West erected statues of Paul and Babe. The huge images that still stand in Bemidji, Minnesota, for example, are listed in the U.S. National Register of Historic Places.

was also known to pull the kinks, or curves, out of a logging road, making it straight!

Paul and Babe were practically inseparable and did some of their greatest work together. As one version of their story tells it, "Paul and Babe were a good team [and] no feat of strength or courage was beyond them. No obstacles ever stumped them. Paul could cut down acres of timber single-handedly in just a few minutes by tying his huge ax to the end of a long rope and swinging it in circles. Babe could haul the logs away as fast as Paul could cut them."[41]

Concrete sculptures of the legendary Paul Bunyan and his blue ox Babe on the shore of Lake Bemidji in Minnesota.

An American Premium on Size

Many of the American hero myths became popular in the 1800s during the period in which pioneers were settling in the ever-moving American frontier. But the origin of the Paul Bunyan stories was an exception. The numerous tall tales and humorous anecdotes associated with that oversized hero first began to take hold in the public mind in the early 1900s. The major place that Paul and his myths occupy in the culture today is a tribute to the power and ingenuity of American advertising. An ad agency in the East created most of his myths, which society proceeded to absorb and revel in.

Paul's backstory began in 1910 when a Michigan journalist named James MacGillivray briefly mentioned the big lumberjack in a Detroit newspaper article. At the time, Paul Bunyan was one of several fictional loggers known only to a handful of lumberjacks in the country's Great Lakes region.

One tale of Paul Bunyan has him swinging his axe and clearing 640 acres of forest.

These men made up tall tales and told them to one another at night over campfires. The vast majority of Americans never heard those tales, and MacGillivray's article reached only a few people in one city.

A couple of years later, a University of Wisconsin student, K. Bernice Stewart, went out to some Wisconsin logging camps and began collecting stories told by the loggers. In 1916 she and her English professor, Homer A. Watt, published a thirteen-page scholarly paper in which some Paul Bunyan tales appeared. Because only a few hundred scholars and students read the paper, even then the Paul Bunyan myth remained unknown to the general public.

It took a logger who later became an advertising executive to introduce one of America's best-loved mythical characters to the country as a whole. That ad man was William B. Laughead. In 1914 and again in 1916, he sent out several thousand pamphlets to the customers of the Red River Lumber Company, a firm he handled. The flyers contained anecdotes about a giant lumberjack, stories designed to entertain the customers. They also contained drawings of Paul, who from then on was the company's mascot or logo. Laughead repeated these same stories, along with others he made up himself, in 1922 in a short book titled *The Marvelous Exploits of Paul Bunyan*. He claimed he came up with the character of Babe, saying in the book's preface, "The names of the supporting characters, including the animals, are inventions by the writer of this version."[42]

This 1922 work marked the first major public debut of the Paul Bunyan myths. From there they spread in a manner nothing less than meteoric, as Paul and Babe became permanent fixtures in storybooks, children's literature, and folklore collections. Paul "grew quick as a twig-snap," Kemp P. Battle writes, "into an American legend. He suited a country that put a premium on size, humor, strength, and zest, and American ingenuity wasted little time expanding his world."[43]

Indeed, culturally speaking, more than anything else it was Paul's astounding bigness that made him a hit with Americans. Although the terms *extra large* and *supersize* were fairly recently coined, their sentiments have been part

Johnny Appleseed in Myth and Reality

One of the most famous American hero myths featured a kindly individual named Johnny Appleseed. Although some of his exploits were indeed fictional or exaggerated, his character was based on a real person—nurseryman and conservationist John Chapman. Born in Leominster, Massachusetts, in 1774, he was the son of Nathaniel Chapman, who fought under George Washington in the American Revolution. Contrary to the popular myth, John Chapman did not plant huge orchards of apple trees. Rather, he created individual nurseries containing apple tree seedlings. Local people in the places to which he traveled—Ohio, Pennsylvania, Indiana, and Illinois—then bought and planted the seedlings. Chapman was also a missionary of the New Church, a small Christian denomination started by Emanuel Swedenborg. When John Chapman died in 1845, he left an estate containing more than 1,200 acres (486ha) of apple nurseries. Over time he became such a renowned folk hero that many storybooks and films described his adventures, some real and many fabricated. Walt Disney's charming 1948 animated film *Melody Time* included a long tribute to Johnny Appleseed.

The legend of Johnny Appleseed is based on John Chapman, a nurseryman and conservationist who lived from 1774 to 1847.

of American social custom for much longer. In a nation obsessed with size, strength, and being first, Paul Bunyan was a fitting addition to a growing band of national folk heroes. As a result, as one expert observer puts it, he came to "maintain a place in the hearts of our country's children and adults alike."[44]

A Supercowboy

During roughly the same period in which the Paul Bunyan tales were taking root in American folklore, myths about another bigger-than-life frontier character were gaining widespread popularity. In this case the hero in question—Pecos Bill—was a supercowboy rather than a superlumberjack. The exact origins of the Pecos Bill tales are still somewhat disputed. Some authorities claim that these stories were originally spun by real cowboys during cattle drives across the vast American plains in the mid- to late 1800s. One possible twist on this explanation is that the cowboys based their fictional character on a real one—William Shaffer. Shaffer was a Civil War engineer who later gained a reputation as a rough, tough cowboy in Texas in the years following the conflict.

Another theory about Pecos Bill's origins is that a writer for *Century Magazine*, Edward O'Reilly, invented the character. O'Reilly's first versions of Bill's adventures appeared in the magazine in 1917. These and other yarns about Bill were collected into a book, *The Saga of Pecos Bill*, in 1923.

O'Reilly definitely did more to popularize Pecos Bill than anyone else in the twentieth century. However, he may not have created the character out of the thin air. Still another hypothesis is that he based his version of Bill on Texas cowboy William Shaffer or the main character in the tales told by cowboys in the late nineteenth century, or both.

Preposterous but Charming Tales

Wherever the concept for the tall tales about Pecos Bill originated, once they gained wide circulation in the country they became almost instant favorites in books about American folklore. In his fictional world, Bill was born in 1830 of pioneer parents. When he was still a baby, the family wagon was ambling along the prairie when it hit a bump and he fell out, unbeknownst to his parents. In the years that followed, he was raised by coyotes. In fact, he actually thought he *was* a coyote, until his human brother found him years later and convinced him he was really a person.

Thereafter, he became a cowboy called Pecos Bill and spawned dozens of truly tall tales. One of the many modern retellers of his life summarizes a few of these preposterous but charming legends:

> Bill grew to be much bigger than most men. He wrestled and rode mountain lions, used rattlesnakes as lassos, and fought grizzly bears with his bare hands. . . . He invented the rope lasso and six-shooter and gained a reputation for killing bad guys. . . . One day a tornado appeared on the horizon. When the twister approached, Bill jumped on it and rode it like a bucking bronco. In an effort to shake Bill, the tornado [spit out rain] so hard that it carved out the Grand Canyon. Bill finally fell off in California, hitting the ground with such force that he formed Death Valley.[45]

Pecos Bill embodies the American myth of the cowboy as a hero.

Like Paul Bunyan, Pecos Bill had a faithful animal companion—his horse, the Widow Maker, also called Lightning. The steed earned the name Widow Maker because he was so ornery. He violently tossed anyone and everyone who tried to ride him off his back, except of course for Bill. Even Bill's girlfriend, Slue-Foot Sue, could not stay on that huge, powerful horse. It was said that after the horse threw her off and she hit the ground, she started bouncing higher and higher until eventually her head hit the moon.

Calamity Jane

Born in 1852 in Princeton, Missouri, Martha Jane Cannary had as many tall tales about her exploits in the American West as any frontiersman. She had a reputation as a hard-drinking, rowdy, foul-mouthed ruffian. But she was also known as a generous, kindhearted woman who was never mean-spirited.

Even Bill's death was big and outrageous. According to the Texas State Historical Association, the way he died

is a matter of controversy. Some cowboys say that he died from drinking fishhooks with his whiskey and nitroglycerin [a liquid so unstable that shaking it can cause it to explode]. Others insist that he died laughing at [city] dudes who called themselves cowboys. Whatever the mode of his death, Pecos Bill exists in cowboy folklore as a hyperbole [exaggeration] of the endurance, enterprise and other qualities required of cowboys.[46]

Indeed, one of the major reasons that Pecos Bill remains so popular is that he embodies the long-cherished myth of the American cowboy. An important offshoot of the legendary American West itself, the cowboy myth views that character type as more admirable and impressive than real cowboys usually were. According to an article about American frontier myths in the British newspaper the *Guardian*:

To this day, the great false beliefs about cowboys prevail: that they were [all] brave, generous, unselfish men; that the west was "won" by noble white American pioneers and staunch American soldiers fighting the red Indian foe; [and] that frontier justice was rough but fair. These absurd but solidly rooted fantasies cannot be [eliminated]. People believe in and identify themselves with these myths and will scratch and kick to maintain their Western self-image. The rest of the country and the world believes in the heroic myth because the tourism bureau will never let anyone forget it.[47]

The legends about Pecos Bill take these "fantasies" of the American cowboy myth to a ridiculous but highly entertaining extreme. In so doing they reinforce that myth for people who still hold it dear. In this way Bill and his wild antics reflect a deeply ingrained aspect of American culture, one that persists despite the fact that the old West now exists only in movies and people's imaginations.

Pecos Bill Learns His True Identity

Among the more charming stories about Pecos Bill is the one in which he discovered that he was human, not a coyote. According to one modern storyteller:

Bill spent seventeen years living like a coyote until one day a cowboy rode by on his horse. Some say the cowboy was one of Bill's brothers. Whoever he was, he took one look at Bill and asked, "What are you?"

Bill was not used to human language. At first, he could not say anything. The cowboy repeated his question. This time, Bill said, "varmint."

That is a word used for any kind of wild animal.

"No you aren't," said the cowboy.

"Yes, I am," said Bill. "I have fleas."

"Lots of people have fleas," said the cowboy. "You don't have a tail."

"Yes, I do," said Bill.

"Show it to me then," the cowboy said.

Bill looked at his backside and realized that he did not have a tail like the other coyotes. "Well, what am I then?" asked Bill.

"You're a cowboy! So start acting like one!" the cowboy cried out. Well that was all Bill needed to hear. He said goodbye to his coyote friends and left to join the world of humans.

Quoted in Voice of America. "Pecos Bill." Transcript, November 28, 2009. http://learningenglish.voanews.com/content/a-23-2009-11-28-voa3-83144122/117096.html.

The Awe-Inspiring Railroads

Still another important feature of American frontier lore was the construction of the first railroads. These iron-railed transportation links connected the East to the West and dramatically reduced the time it took to travel across the frontier. Moreover, at the time, they were seen as an example of American technology and ingenuity on the cutting edge. Thanks to these qualities, along with their sheer size as engineering projects, the railroads provided much material for the spinning of new myths, as researcher Nora Carter confirms:

> The railroad was an awe inspiring thing to see to the people of the frontier. This is reflected in the many myths and legends that surround [the early] railways, stations, and tracks, even to this day. The railroads brought people from many walks of life together mixing cultures and traditions, creating a brand new hodgepodge of mythology involving elements from many cultures.[48]

Among these cultures was that of the African Americans who had been brought to the Americas against their will and forced to work as slaves. University of Nebraska scholar William G. Thomas explains:

> Slavery is often thought of as a primarily agricultural phenomenon [because so many black slaves worked on southern plantations], but thousands of enslaved blacks worked on the railroads right up to and during the Civil War, grading lines, building bridges, and blasting tunnels. They hauled timber, cut wood, and shoveled dirt and stone. Skilled slaves, especially blacksmiths, stone masons, and carpenters, worked on the railroads too. Railroad companies and contractors hired slaves by the hundreds; they also purchased slaves directly, in lots of 50 or more. In fact, by the 1850s, the South's railroad companies could be counted among the largest slaveholders in their regions.[49]

Because many African Americans worked on railroad construction as slaves and, later, for very low wages, they needed a champion to tell their tale. That champion was the mythical John Henry, the steel-driving man.

African Americans also worked on the railroads after they gained their freedom in the 1860s. Although no longer slaves, many were treated little or no better than slaves. Their pay was very low, and they worked under extremely difficult and sometimes inhumane conditions.

John Henry Accepts the Challenge

Of the tales that emerged from the toils of the black railroad workers in that period, none became more famous and enduring than that of John Henry, the "steel-driving man." Some experts think he was an exaggerated memory of a real African American worker who was born shortly before the Civil War. The story goes that John Henry was employed by the wealthy Chesapeake and Ohio (C&O) Railroad. As a "hammer man," his job was to break up large rocks that blocked the planned route of the new tracks. Raising his huge sledgehammer, he pounded it into a steel spike that in turn shattered the rocks, which was clearly backbreaking, monotonous work.

One day the railroad gang came up against Big Bend Mountain in West Virginia. The bosses decided it would be too expensive to lay tracks all the way around the mountain, so they informed the workers that they would have to tunnel straight through the obstacle. The job took close to one thousand men nearly three years to finish. Throughout the ordeal, John Henry repeatedly demonstrated that he was the strongest, fastest, and most efficient driller working for the C&O.

The Real John Henry

Carlene Hempel, of the University of North Carolina–Chapel Hill, offers what little is known about the real, historical figure John Henry, a poor former slave who spent his adult life working in railroad gangs.

> The story of John Henry, told mostly through ballads and work songs, traveled from coast to coast as the railroads drove west during the 19th Century. And in time, it has become timeless. . . .
>
> From what we know, John Henry was born a slave in the 1840s or 1850s in North Carolina or Virginia. He grew to stand 6 feet tall, 200 pounds—a giant in that day. He had an immense appetite, and an even greater capacity for work. He carried a beautiful baritone voice, and was a favorite banjo player to all who knew him.

> One among a legion of blacks just freed from the war, John Henry went to work rebuilding the Southern states whose territory had been ravaged by the Civil War. The period became known as the Reconstruction, a reunion of the nation under one government after the Confederacy lost the war. . . . Thousands upon thousands of [African American] men [entered] the workforce, mostly in deplorable conditions and for poor wages.
>
> As far as anyone can determine, John Henry was hired as a steel-driver for the C&O Railroad, a wealthy company that was extending its line from the Chesapeake Bay to the Ohio Valley.

Carlene Hempel. "The Man—Facts, Fiction and Themes." John Henry: The Steel Driving Man. www.ibiblio.org /john_henry/analysis.html.

No sooner had the tunnel been created than a salesman arrived in camp. He had with him a big, imposing-looking drilling machine—the latest, most advanced invention to come out of the industrialized East, he bragged. He claimed this contraption could easily out-drill any steel driver in the C&O's crew. A number of drillers believed the machine could *not* outwork them, but none of them had the nerve to prove it by going one-on-one in a contest with the scary-looking gadget.

In contrast, John Henry saw the idea of competing with the machine "as a challenge," myth teller Shirley Love writes. "So a contest was planned between John and the steam-drill." The next day, carrying two 20-pound (9kg) hammers, he took his place beside the automated driller. At a given signal, Love continues,

> the man and machine squared off. After about a half hour, John had drilled two seven foot holes for a total of fourteen feet and the machine had drilled only one nine-foot hole. The railroad men shouted and cheered at John's victory, but suddenly the mighty man fell to the ground exhausted, and there he died. The myth says that if you walk to the edge of the Big Bend tunnel you can sometimes hear the sound of two twenty pound hammers inside, drilling their way to victory over the machine.[50]

A Hero on Two Levels

From a cultural perspective, John Henry's inspiring myth works on two different levels. First, from an African American standpoint, the tale represents a metaphor, or symbolic example, of a black man challenging a repressive system run by whites. To the company owners and other well-to-do whites, John Henry was a good worker, but also socially and morally inferior to them. The machine represented the best product that white society could manufacture. So when John competed with and beat the machine, he showed that African Americans were every bit as worthy as whites, even if the bosses and their friends refused to acknowledge that truth.

On a larger, more universal level, John Henry's great feat focused people's attention on a problem that began in

A statue in a park in Talcott, West Virginia, commemorates John Henry's work on the C & O Railroad.

the Industrial Revolution of his era and still persists today. Namely, is it desirable, as well as morally right, for machines to replace human workers? In the late 1800s and throughout the 1900s, American society debated the issue as advanced machines increasingly took over jobs formerly done by people. In this respect, the myth is "about power," researcher Carlene Hempel states, the power of people to physically accomplish things. It calls attention to "the individual, raw strength" of a human being, a quality "that no system" and no machine can or should "take from a man."[51]

Ultimately, therefore, John Henry is both an African American hero and a human hero. In addition, in one essential way he resembles Paul Bunyan, Pecos Bill, and numerous other classic mythical American heroes. He and they are the embodiment of strength, vigor, and independent achievement, just like the youthful, dynamic nation that gave rise to them.

CHAPTER 5

The Myths in Pop Culture

Many of the beloved American myths that developed during the course of colonial and early U.S. history long remained folktales told by families beside the fireplace or to children at bedtime. Yet these same stories often became much more than simple examples of enjoyable storytelling. One by one, they made their way into popular culture. Frequently called "pop" or "mass" culture for short, it is the sum of historical events and figures, customs, ideas, attitudes, and visual images shared by the vast majority of Americans.

American myths entered (and continue to enter) pop culture through a wide range of media. They included almanacs, newspapers, dime novels (short, semifictional novels that were most popular in the 1800s), standard novels, magazines, paintings, songs, and eventually radio, television, movies, and the Internet. As an expert observer states:

By the mid-[1800s], it was increasingly clear that the divisions perceived to exist between folk culture and mass culture were beginning to be blurred. . . . All-American heroes such as Davy Crockett, [John Henry, and others] . . . were mythologized through almanacs, newspapers, and dime novels. . . . The frontier and the

West continued to be a source of fascination well into the twentieth century as ... [numerous] Western characters ... were, through the medium of the moving picture, [embedded] forever within the nation's consciousness.[52]

Indeed, although many forms of media have helped to entrench the myths in pop culture, movies were and continue to be the most admired, trendy, and influential medium. One reason for this is that film is a multidimensional art form. It combines creative elements, including writing, directing, acting, photography, visual design, music, and more in one neat package. Also, millions of people are exposed to a given movie in the space of only a few days or weeks. So when a myth—for example one about a pirate's ghost, an American werewolf, or a frontier hero—is depicted in a movie, it cements that tale into the public consciousness in a big way.

Walt Disney brought stories of Davy Crockett to life for a new generation of Americans in the 1950s.

Trophies Named for the Giant Logger

One of the more unexpected cultural manifestations of the Paul Bunyan tales was the adoption of trophies based on the myth by college football teams. One of these awards is known as Paul Bunyan's Ax. Every year since 1948 the University of Minnesota Golden Gophers and the University of Wisconsin Badgers have competed for the trophy. The winner of each game has its name inscribed on the ax's handle, which is 6 feet (1.8m) long. By tradition, if the team that won the previous year wins, its players carry the ax around the field in a victory lap. In similar fashion, each year since 1953 the University of Michigan Wolverines and the Michigan State University Spartans play a football game in hopes of winning the Paul Bunyan–Governor of Michigan Trophy.

Victorious Wisconsin football players carry off the Paul Bunyan's Ax trophy after defeating the University of Minnesota.

Lost Cities, Islands, and Plateaus

A clear example of this process can be seen in the cultural absorption of the mythical lost city (or kingdom or island) into American pop culture. At first, it happened mainly through poems, novels, and other forms of literature. The lost city or realm of El Dorado, for instance, was used by the great seventeenth-century English writer John Milton in his 1667 epic poem *Paradise Lost*. Milton depicted God taking the first man, Adam, to the summit of a mountain and showing him a series of paradises and utopias, one of them El Dorado in the Americas.

Later, in *Candide*, a brilliant short novel penned by the French writer Voltaire in 1759, a brave knight searches for and finds El Dorado. Also, American writer Edgar Allan Poe's 1849 poem "Eldorado" references that legendary American kingdom. A mythical place no less uncharted and magical than El Dorado was created by English writer Arthur Conan Doyle for his 1912 novel *The Lost World*. This classic work depicts a modern expedition discovering prehistoric beasts on a lost American plateau. In addition, American novelist James Hilton invented an unknown, miraculous mountain valley—Shangri-La, where people age unnaturally slowly—in his 1933 book *Lost Horizon*.

All of these poems and novels were literary successes in their own eras and over time built up loyal audiences of up to hundreds of thousands of readers. But it was not until most of them were made into movies in the twentieth century that they reached audiences of many millions and became widely recognized cultural classics. Particularly popular were the mythical plateaus, valleys, and islands that were visited by awe-struck outsiders in the course of these tales. Doyle's *Lost World*, for instance, was made into numerous feature films,

Arthur Conan Doyle's 1912 novel The Lost World *is about a lost plateau inhabited by prehistoric beasts somewhere in the Americas. It has been the inspiration for many films and TV shows. This scene is from the 1925 feature film.*

including versions in 1925, 1960, 1992, and 1998. The novel also gained widespread popularity through close to a dozen lower-budget television and radio productions.

Equally popular was a lost island reminiscent of Doyle's lost plateau in the three versions of *King Kong* (1933, 1976, and 2005). Called Skull Island, it, like the plateau, was infested with prehistoric monsters, as well as the giant ape named in the film's title. Hilton's *Lost Horizon* also found enormous new audiences thanks to the two movies made from it in 1937 and 1973.

"The Jersey Devil Made Me Do It"

The classic American myths of monsters also initially entered mass culture though various literary works and later reached larger audiences thanks to movie versions. The memory of the Jersey Devil, for example, spawned in colonial days, was long perpetuated by word of mouth and short tales included in folktale and horror anthologies. In the twentieth century a number of full-length books appeared, most of them presenting sightings of the monster by a variety of witnesses in an attempt to show it might be a real creature. Probably the best-known example is *The Jersey Devil*, a 1987 volume by James F. McCloy and Ray Miller. The publisher made a strongly worded claim, saying, "The authors point out that while a few appearances [of the creature] have been outright fraud and other sightings of it have likely been the result of mass hysteria, this creature has been seen by enough sane, sober, and responsible citizens to keep the possibility of its existence alive and tantalizing."[53]

Tantalizing or not, this and other books about the monster of the Pine Barrens were far from best sellers, and as late as the 1990s a majority of Americans outside of the Northeast had never heard of the Jersey Devil. This changed with the release of a major feature film about the creature in 2002. Titled *13th Child: Legend of the Jersey Devil*, it starred Oscar winner Cliff Robertson

Hockey Adopts a Monster

One of the Jersey Devil's entries into pop culture was its adoption by a well-known New Jersey hockey team that began playing in the Eastern Hockey League in 1964. It called itself the Jersey Devils until 1982, when it became the New Jersey Devils.

(who also cowrote the script). The film tells the story of a present-day local district attorney who investigates a series of grisly murders. He soon begins to wonder if the culprit is human or if it might be the infamous monster associated with the nearby Pine Barrens.

Another theatrical film about the monster—appropriately titled *The Jersey Devil*—was released in 2005. It goes back to the original myth about the infamous Leeds family and dramatizes the terrifying moments when Jane Leeds gave birth to the monster. In the movie, she hopes her hideous offspring will get revenge on the townspeople for their mean-spirited treatment of her. A third Jersey Devil movie was released in 2012. Titled *The Barrens* and directed by Darren Lynn Bousman, it follows the exploits of a man who takes his family on a camping trip in the Pine Barrens and becomes convinced that they are being stalked by the frightening Jersey Devil.

Over the years, the creature appeared in numerous TV shows as well. One was an episode from the first season of the widely popular *X-Files*, which followed the adventures of two FBI agents who encounter diverse kinds of bizarre phenomena. In the episode, they discover that the creature is actually one of a group of feral people living in the remote stretches of the Pine Barrens. Other television shows that tackled the Jersey Devil included *Paranormal State*, *Extreme Ghostbusters* (in a episode amusingly titled "The Jersey Devil Made Me Do It"), and *Monster Quest*.

Those Hairy Mythical Beasts

Several other popular American monsters have also become regular characters in pop culture through both books and movies. Sasquatch (or Bigfoot), for instance, is the subject of numerous nonfiction books whose authors are convinced that the creature is a real animal. One of the earliest and still most important of the books was *Abominable Snowmen: Legend Come to Life; The Story of Sub-humans on Five Continents from the Early Ice Age Until Today*. The 1961 work was written by a well-known investigator of strange phenomena, Ivan T. Sanderson. Because he was a trained naturalist, he lent a touch of credibility to ongoing books

Sasquatch Comes to Town

Most books about Sasquatch discuss sightings of the mythical creature in remote wilderness areas. In contrast, the groundbreaking 2009 book *Impossible Visits: The Inside Story of Interactions with Sasquatch at Habitation Sites* by Christopher Noel, cites reports of the monster in towns and other inhabited places.

and articles about cryptozoology, the study of animals whose existence has yet to be proven. Sanderson proposed that the hairy creatures of the Sasquatch myths might be members of a strain or tribe of early humans that still survives in remote areas of the United States and elsewhere.

Dozens of other books about Sasquatch were published in the late twentieth century. But as was the case with other mythical monsters, the written material never drew as many enthusiasts as most of the movies did. The first film versions, including *The Snow Creature* (1954), were low budget, and the costume and makeup they employed for the actor portraying the monster were not very convincing. So these attempts to portray Sasquatch did not do very well at the box office.

More realistic and much more financially successful were several Sasquatch films made in the 1970s and 1980s. The first of these, *The Legend of Boggy Creek*, released in 1972, became a sort of cult classic of the genre and spawned several sequels. Also popular at the box office were *Creature from Black Lake* (1976) and *Sasquatch: The Legend of Bigfoot* (1977).

Most popular of all was *Harry and the Hendersons*, a 1987 comic takeoff on the Sasquatch myth starring John Lithgow. His character is a family man who receives a nocturnal visit from Sasquatch, played by Kevin Peter Hall. Because the creature is gentle and lovable rather than violent and frightening, the family adopts it, leading to a number of humorous consequences. That Sasquatch films had come a long way since the less-than-credible *Snow Creature* was shown when *Harry* won an Academy Award for best makeup design.

Those other hairy mythical beasts—American werewolves—also proved popular in books and movies. One of the best novels featuring werewolves inhabiting parts of the United States is horror master Dean Koontz's 1989 horror-murder-mystery *Midnight*. Other well-written novels that further developed the American werewolf myth were Gary Brandner's *The Howling* (1986), Whitley Strieber's *The Wolfen* (1988), and Paul D. Brazill's *Drunk on the Moon* (2011). Notable movie outings for American werewolves were *The Wolfman* (1941), with Lon Chaney Jr. as the man who becomes a monster when the moon is full; *I Was a Teen-aged Werewolf* (1957), with a young Michael Landon in the title role; the semicomic *An American Werewolf in London* (1981); *The Howling* (1981), with some very realistic and

Sasquatch, or Bigfoot, has been the subject of a wide variety of films from horror to comedy. The 1987 movie Harry and the Hendersons *portrays Bigfoot as a lovable member of a human family.*

scary wolfmen; and the recent *Twilight* films, with their clan of Native American werewolves who have a running feud with some local vampires.

Ghost Myths in American Culture

Ghost myths, including some of the earliest ghost ship tales from colonial times, are still very much a part of American culture. One of the most enduring ghost ship stories among Americans is that of the *Flying Dutchman*. Its popularity can be seen by the wide array of cultural venues it has found its way into. For example, the Nickelodeon children's TV show *SpongeBob SquarePants* features a pirate-like character called the Flying Dutchman.

The original *Flying Dutchman*, of course, was not a man but rather a vessel condemned to wander the seas. Its spooky but also romantic image inspired many American artists, among them noted painters Albert Ryder and Howard Pyle. Ryder's exquisite version of the famous ghost ship still hangs in the Smithsonian American Art Museum in Washington, D.C. Pyle's version, done on a large canvas more than 6 feet (1.8m) high, depicts a young sailor aboard the ship, his expression revealing his longing for the ship's curse to somehow end.

The *Flying Dutchman* made a number of appearances in American literature as well. One of the most memorable examples is Edgar Allan Poe's 1833 short story "MS. Found in a Bottle." It tells about a shipwrecked sailor who ends up on a mysterious vessel with a very odd-acting crew, an obvious reference to the *Flying Dutchman* myth. The latter is also the basis for *The Flying Dutchman on Tappan Sea*, an 1855 fable by Washington Irving, author of *Rip Van Winkle* and *The Legend of Sleepy Hollow*.

A memorable movie version of the myth of the *Flying Dutchman* was the 1951 Hollywood film *Pandora and the Flying Dutchman*. It starred James Mason as a Dutch ship captain who is

A Monster Strikes It Rich

The 1972 film *The Legend of Boggy Creek* cost only a bit more than one hundred thousand dollars to make, yet has so far grossed more than $20 million in revenues, including profits from theater showings and videotape and DVD rentals. It generated four sequels.

allowed to walk on land once every seven years in hopes of finding a woman who will love him. His love interest—the woman who finally does come to love him, thereby breaking the curse—was played by the then popular Ava Gardner. Another movie appearance of the *Flying Dutchman* is in the Disney *Pirates of the Caribbean* films—a ghost ship piloted by a cursed, hideous-looking captain and crew.

Artist Albert Pinkham Ryder's Flying Dutchman *can be seen at the Smithsonian's American Art Museum in Washington, D.C.*

Paul Bunyan Meets the Arts

American folk heroes such as Paul Bunyan and John Henry have been immortalized not only in their original myths, but also in a range of artistic media, including music and film. One of the first cultural expressions of Paul Bunyan's legend was a 1941 operetta (short or light opera). The music was composed by Benjamin Britten, and the libretto (play with dialogue) was by noted Anglo-American poet W.H. Auden. The mythical basis and theme of this melodic, appealing work were summarized by Auden himself in a preface to the libretto. Modern interest in Paul's myth, he wrote,

> is a reflection of the cultural problems that occur during the first stage of every civilization, the stage of colonization of the land and the conquest of nature. The operetta, therefore, begins [when] America is still a virgin forest and Paul Bunyan has not been born, and ends with a Christmas party at which he bids farewell . . . because now he is no longer needed. External physical nature has been mastered, and for this very reason can no longer dictate to men what they should do. Now their task is one of their human relations with each other and, for this, a collective mythical figure is no [longer of any] use.[54]

Oliver Platt as Paul Bunyan sits atop his blue ox Babe in a scene from the 1995 movie Tall Tale: The Unbelievable Adventures of Pecos Bill.

The operetta's principal shortcoming was that, as a live stage play, it was able to reach and entertain only a modest number of people. By contrast, several later filmed versions of the Paul Bunyan legend reached much wider audiences. The first and still most famous was a Walt Disney animated

short film released to movie theaters in 1958. Paul's voice was contributed by the late character actor Thurl Ravenscroft.

Another movie appearance by Paul Bunyan was in a 1995 live action Disney production—the full-length feature film *Tall Tale*. This time Paul was portrayed by popular modern actor Oliver Platt. These films, along with scattered television portrayals of Paul Bunyan, introduced whole new generations of young people to his still-expanding myth.

"An Exuberant Folklore"

Pecos Bill and John Henry also received numerous filmic treatments over the years, making them household names across the United States and often well beyond. As in the case of several other American folk heroes, Walt Disney led the way. His 1948 animated short film based on the Pecos Bill legends was a critical and financial success. Narrated by the then widely popular American cowboy star Roy Rogers, it set the standard for later cinematic renditions of the myth. (Years later, when Disneyland in California and Disney World in Florida were built, they featured the Pecos Bill Tall Tale Inn and Cafe, located in Frontierland.)

Disney later followed up by including Pecos Bill in the 1995 movie *Tall Tale*. Bill was portrayed in the film by the late actor Patrick Swayze (famous for his roles in films such as *Dirty Dancing*, *Ghost*, and *Point Break*). *Tall Tale* also featured as a character the courageous railroad worker John Henry, played by Roger Aaron Brown.

As it turned out, *Tall Tale* was not the only cultural niche that Paul Bunyan, Pecos Bill, and John Henry shared. In 1996 the U.S. Postal Service issued new 32-cent stamps as tributes to them. Usually only very well-known and respected people or characters are honored this way. So the stamps showed how far these legendary characters had wormed their way into the public eye and national heart.

As the years go by, it is likely Americans will continue to recognize their native folk heroes and enjoy their stories. American tales of lost cities, monsters, and ghosts, and those depicting bigger-than-life folk heroes, are likely to endure for many generations and centuries to come. This is

"John Henry Went Upon the Mountain"

The myth of John Henry has inspired a large number of songs over the years. This is one of several that are in the public domain:

> John Henry went upon the
> mountain,
> Looked down on the other side.
> Oh the mountain was so tall, John
> Henry watched it fall.
> Laid down his hammer and he
> cried.
> Lord, Lord, laid down his hammer
> and cried.
>
> John Henry had a pretty little
> wife,
> Her name was Liza Jane.
> John Henry took sick, had to go
> to bed,
> John draw steel like a man.

> John Henry said to his Captain,
> I want to go to bed.
> Fix me a pallet, I wanna lay down,
> But let it roll in my head,
> Lord, Lord, let it roll in my head.

"John Henry." Bluegrass Songs. Radford University. www .radford.edu/~bluegrass/songs/johnhenry.html.

The mythical figure of John Henry was immortalized on a 1996 U.S. postage stamp.

partly because they are so vivid, alive, appealing, and often humorous. "America has an exuberant folklore," Kemp P. Battle points out, "a tradition of wit that possesses the rare capacity to reinvent itself over and over." In this respect, he says, Paul Bunyan, Davy Crockett, Pecos Bill, and the others are "American creation[s], blood and bone made from a marvelous spirit that shall endure forever and ever."[55]

Introduction: Teaching People About Themselves

1. Oracle Think Quest. "American Heroes." http://library.thinkquest.org/05aug/00212/american.html.
2. Gilbert Highet. *Poets in the Landscape*. New York: Random House, 1957, p. 540.

Chapter 1: Legendary Lost Cities

3. James Harpur and Jennifer Westwood. *Atlas of Legendary Places*. New York: Grove, 1997, p. 6.
4. Quoted in *Archives of the West*. "The Journey of Coronado." PBS. www.pbs.org/weta/thewest/resources/archives/one/corona2.htm.
5. Nelson B. Keyes. *The American Frontier*. Whitefish, MT: Kessinger, 2009, p. 35.
6. Quoted in John Bowman et al. *American Folklore and Legend*. Pleasantville, NY: Reader's Digest, 1978, p. 61.
7. Quoted in José Toribio Medina. *The Discovery of the Amazon*. Translated by H.C. Heaton. New York: AMS, 1970, pp. 391–392.
8. Henry J. Sage. "The American Colonial Experience: Introduction," April 20, 2002. http://homepage.ntlworld.com/chris.thorns/resources/Translations/Colonial Intro.pdf.
9. Quoted in Charles Pierce. *Idiot America: How Stupidity Became a Virtue in the Land of the Free*. New York: Random House, 2010, p. 19.
10. Quoted in Pierce. *Idiot America*, p. 19.
11. Ignatius Donnelly. *Atlantis: The Antediluvian World*. Charleston, SC: Bibliobazaar, 2007, p. 337.
12. Keith Fitzpatrick-Matthews and James Doeser. "Atlantis." *Bad Archaeology* (blog). www.badarchaeology.com/?page_id=481.
13. Alexis de Tocqueville. *Democracy in America*. Edited by Richard D. Heffner. New York: Penguin, 1984, p. 54.

Chapter 2: Monsters on the Loose

14. W. Scott Poole. *Monsters in America*. Waco, TX: Baylor University Press, 2011, p. 4.
15. Quoted in Bowman et al. *American Folklore and Legend*, p. 246.
16. B.A. Botkin, ed. *A Treasury of New England Folklore*. New York: Bonanza, 1988, pp. 195–196.

17. Virginia Haviland. *North American Legends*. New York: Collins, 1981, p. 185.
18. S.E. Schlosser. "Birth of the Jersey Devil." American Folklore. http://americanfolklore.net/folklore/2010/07/birth_of_the_jersey_devil.html.
19. Troy Taylor. "Unexplained America: The Jersey Devil—Legend or Truth?" American Hauntings. www.prairieghosts.com/jerseydevil.html.
20. Charles M. Skinner. *Myths and Legends of Our Own Land*. Vol. 2. New York: Cosimo, 2007, p. 139.
21. Ben Radford. "Bigfoot at 50: Evaluating a Half-Century of Bigfoot Evidence." Committee for Skeptical Inquiry. www.csicop.org/si/show/bigfoot_at_50_evaluating_a_half-century_of_bigfoot_evidence.
22. Poole. *Monsters in America*, book jacket.
23. Laurie Essig. "Why We Wanted to Believe Botox Mom Was a Real Monster." *Love, Inc* (blog), *Psychology Today*, May 21, 2011. www.psychologytoday.com/blog/love-inc/201105/why-we-wanted-believe-botox-mom-was-real-monster.
24. Poole. *Monsters in America*, p. viii.
25. Poole. *Monsters in America*, pp. 4–5.

Chapter 3: Ghosts Haunt the Living

26. Botkin. *A Treasury of New England Folklore*, p. 178.
27. Kemp P. Battle, ed. *Great American Folklore: Legends, Tales, Ballads, and Superstitions from All Across America*. Garden City, NY: Doubleday, 1989, p. 302.
28. Quoted in Bowman et al. *American Folklore and Legend*, p. 19.
29. Battle. *Great American Folklore*, p. 302.
30. S.T. Livermore. *Block Island*. Hartford, CT: Case, Lockwood, and Brainard, 1882, pp. 93–94.
31. National Maritime Museum. "Pirates." www.rmg.co.uk/explore/sea-and-ships/facts/ships-and-seafarers/pirates.
32. Southeastern Ghosts and Hauntings. "Ghost of Blackbeard, Ocracoke Island, North Carolina." http://southeasternghosts.blogspot.com/2012/05/ghost-of-blackbeard-ocracoke-island.html.
33. S.E. Schlosser. "Black Bartelmy's Ghost." American Folklore. http://americanfolklore.net/folklore/2010/07/black_bartelmys_ghost.html.
34. L'Aura Muller. "The Ghosts of Ringwood Manor." New Jersey History's Mysteries. www.njhm.com/ringwoodmanor.htm.
35. Jill Stefko. "Ringwood Manor's Controversial Ghosts." Suite 101, March 28, 2009. http://suite101.com/article/ringwood-manor-ghosts-a105587.
36. Emma Barden. "Why Do We Believe in Ghosts?" *Eulogy*. www.eulogymagazine.co.uk/#/why-do-we-believe-in-ghosts/4549881020.

Chapter 4: Tall Tales About Heroes

37. B.A. Botkin, ed. *A Treasury of American Folklore*. New York: Bonanza, 1993, p. 2.
38. Diana Chike. "Tall Tale Heroes of the American Frontier." University of North Carolina–Chapel Hill, April 18, 2004. www.ils.unc.edu /dpr/path/talltales/index.html.
39. Botkin. *A Treasury of American Folklore*, p. 3.
40. S.E. Schlosser. "Birth of Paul Bunyan." American Folklore. http://americanfolklore.net/folk lore/2010/07/the_birth_of_paul _bunyan.html.
41. Bemidji Chamber of Commerce. "Paul Bunyan Tales." www.visit bemidji.com/bemidji/paultales .html.
42. William B. Laughead. *The Marvelous Exploits of Paul Bunyan*. Project Gutenberg. www.gutenberg.org /files/5800/5800-h/5800-h.htm.
43. Battle. *Great American Folklore*, p. 601.
44. Juniper Russo. "Paul Bunyan: A Fakelore Hoax." Yahoo! Voices, February 20, 2009. http://voices .yahoo.com/paul-bunyan-fakelore -hoax-2668564.html?cat=37.
45. Quoted in Myths Encyclopedia: Myths and Legends of the World. "Pecos Bill." www.mythencyclope dia.com/Pa-Pr/Pecos-Bill.html.
46. Texas State Historical Association. "Pecos Bill." www.tshaonline.org /handbook/online/articles/lxp01.
47. *Guardian* (Manchester, UK). "How the West Was Spun," June 24, 2005. www.guardian.co.uk/books/2005 /jun/25/featuresreviews.guardian review24.
48. Nora Carver. "A Look at American Frontier Mythology, Part 1." Helium, September 4, 2008. www .helium.com/items/1170551-wild -west-tall-tales-american-myths -american-folklore.
49. William G. Thomas. "Been Workin' on the Railroad." *Opinionator* (blog), *New York Times*, February 10, 2012. http://opinionator.blogs .nytimes.com/2012/02/10/been -workin-on-the-railroad.
50. Shirley Love. "A Look at American Frontier Mythology, Part 2." Helium, February 9, 2010. www .helium.com/items/1736664-folk lore-of-americas-frontier?page=2.
51. Carlene Hempel. "The Man—Facts, Fiction and Themes." John Henry: The Steel Driving Man. www.ibib lio.org/john_henry/analysis.html.

Chapter 5: The Myths in Pop Culture

52. *Dictionary of American History*. "Folklore." Encyclopedia. com. www.encyclopedia.com/doc /1G2-3401801545.html.
53. Quoted in James F. McCloy and Ray Miller. *The Jersey Devil*. Moorestown, NJ: Middle Atlantic, 1987, back cover copy.
54. Quoted in Ellen Pfeifer. "Britten's *Paul Bunyan*." New England Conservatory, March 19, 2012. http:// necmusic.edu/brittens-paul-bun yan.
55. Battle. *Great American Folklore*, p. 602.

Books

Kemp P. Battle, ed. *Great American Folklore: Legends, Tales, Ballads, and Superstitions from All Across America.* Garden City, NY: Doubleday, 1989. One of the better available collections of American folklore, this volume covers a wide range of categories, including pioneer tales, animal stories, tales of the Wild West, ghost stories, and much more.

B.A. Botkin, ed. *A Treasury of American Folklore.* New York: Bonanza, 1993. This is one of the classics of the genre, a huge collection presented by one of the leading American folklorists of the twentieth century.

B.A. Botkin, ed. *A Treasury of New England Folklore.* New York: Bonanza, 1988. Botkin's compilation of New England myths is crammed with little-known tales and anecdotes from that region, along with many better-known ones.

John H. Brunvand. *The Study of American Folklore.* New York: Norton, 1998. The author has produced a very useful, appealing, and easy-to-read overview of most of the better-known American myths and legends.

Stephen Clissold. *The Seven Cities of Cibola.* New York: Potter, 1962. Despite its age, this remains one of the most informative books available on the lore of the famous seven cities.

Andrew Collins. *Gateway to Atlantis: The Search for the Source of a Lost Civilization.* New York: Carroll and Graf, 2000. Collins, who advocates the idea that Atlantis was in the Caribbean, provides an enormous amount of well-researched information about competing Atlantis theories.

Richard Ellis. *Imagining Atlantis.* New York: Random House, 1998. A well-written, carefully researched recent study of Atlantis, including an overview of the many theories about the lost continent's location.

Virginia Haviland. *North American Legends.* New York: Collins, 1981. This well-organized, easy-to-read book contains an excellent section on African American folktales, as well as retellings of the adventures of classic characters like Pecos Bill, Stormalong, and Johnny Appleseed.

W.C. Jameson. *Ozark Tales of Ghosts, Spirits, Hauntings, and Monsters.* Nashville, TN: Goldminds, 2007.

A fun read, this volume contains dozens of retellings of myths about haunted mansions, lake and river monsters, and animal ghosts that originated in the central region of the United States.

David S. Lavender. *De Soto, Coronado, Cabrillo: Explorers of the Northern Mystery*. Washington, DC: National Park Service Division of Publications, 1992. A well-written, informative volume chronicling some of the major European explorers who searched for lost cities in the Americas.

Mary Pope Osborne. *American Tall Tales*. New York: Knopf, 1991. Aimed at younger readers, Osborne's versions of several classic American folktales and legends are well-written and lively.

W. Scott Poole. *Monsters in America*. Waco, TX: Baylor University Press, 2011. This fascinating book takes a detailed look at many of the monsters that Americans have come to know and love over the decades and offers reasons why many people enjoy stories, books, and movies about such scary creatures.

Ellyn Sanna. *North American Folklore: Folk Tales and Legends*. Broomall, PA: Mason Crest, 2003. In a format and writing style intended for young readers, the author covers numerous well-known American myths, including ones about heroes, magic, ghosts, the beginnings of things, and much more.

Alvin Schwartz. *Whoppers: Tall Tales and Other Lies Collected from American Folklore*. New York: HarperCollins, 1975. A very easy-to-read and enjoyable collection of mostly little-known, often humorous American folk stories.

Gus Snedeker. *Heroes, Fools, and Ghosts*. Broomall, PA: Mason Crest, 2012. This brief but solid collection of classic American myths is aimed at grade school readers.

Internet Sources

Willie Drye. "Seven Cities of Cibola Legend Lures Conquistadors." *National Geographic*. http://science.nationalgeographic.com/science/archaeology/seven-cities-of-cibola.

Ed Foxe. "Pirate Myths and Their Origins." Pirate Legends. www.piratesinfo.com/cpi_pirate_myths_pirate_legends_944.asp.

Michael A. Lofaro. "Davy Crockett." Texas State Historical Association. www.tshaonline.org/handbook/online/articles/fcr24.

L'Aura Muller. "The Ghosts of Ringwood Manor." New Jersey History's Mysteries. www.njhm.com/ringwoodmanor.htm.

S.E. Schlosser. "The Headless Horseman." American Folklore. http://americanfolklore.net/folklore/2010/07/the_headless_horseman.html.

S.E. Schlosser. "John Henry: The Steel-Driving Man." American Folklore. http://americanfolklore.net/folklore/2010/07/john_henry.html.

Troy Taylor. "Unexplained America: The Jersey Devil—Legend or Truth?" American Hauntings. www.prairieghosts.com/jerseydevil.html.

Wisconsin Historical Society. "The Peculiar Birth of Paul Bunyan." www.wisconsinhistory.org/odd/archives/003040.asp.

Website

The Conquistadors, **PBS** (www.pbs.org/conquistadors/index.html). The home page of the informative PBS documentary on the great Spanish adventurers and seekers of lost cities, based on the book by popular writer Michael Wood.

INDEX

McCloy, James F., 84
Mendoza, Antonio de, 18, 20
Midnight (Koontz), 86
Milton, John, 82
Monster Quest (TV program), 85
Mothman, 6, 46
"MS. Found in a Bottle" (Poe), 88
Myrtles Plantation, *62*

N
Niza, Marcos de, 18

O
O'Reilly, Edward, 71
Oviedo, Gonzalo Fernández de, 21–22

P
Palatine (ghost ship), 54
Pandora and the Flying Dutchman (film), 88–89
Paradise Lost (Milton), 82
Paranormal State (TV program), 85
Paul Bunyon's Ax, 82, *82*
Pecos Bill, *7*, 65, 71–74, *72*
  in popular culture, 91
Phantom puppies, myth of, 50–51
Pirates, 54–55
  buried treasure and, 59
Pirates of the Caribbean (film), 89
Pizarro, Francisco, 21
Pizarro, Gonzalo, 22–23
Plato, 25
Poe, Edgar Allen, 83, 88
Postel, Guillaume de, 26
Pyle, Howard, 88

Q
Queen Anne's Revenge (pirate ship), 55

R
Railroads, construction of, 75–76
  African Americans working on, *76*
Ray, Miller, 84
Red Dwarf, 45
Ringwood Manor, 61
Ryder, Albert Pinkham, 88, 89

S
The Saga of Pecos Bill (O'Reilly), 71
Sanderson, Ivan T., 85–86
Sandovate, Don, 6, 52
Sasquatch (Bigfoot), *7*, 40, 41, *41*, 43–45, *44*
  in popular culture, 85–86
Sasquatch: The Legend of Bigfoot (film), 86
Sauson, Guillaume, 26
Sauson, Nicholas, 26
Sea Serpent of 1817, *7*, 32, *33*
Sea serpents, 32–37, *33*
Seven Cities of Cibola, 13, 15–17
  Coronado's expedition to find, 18–20
Shaffer, William, 71
The Snow Creature (film), 86
Spence, Lewis, 26, 28
SpongeBob SquarePants (TV program), 88
Stewart, K. Bernice, 69
Stormalong, Alfred, 34
Strieber, Whitley, 87
Swedenborg, Emanuel, 70

T

Tall Tale (film), *90,* 91
Teach, Edward. *See* Blackbeard
Texas State Historical Association, 73
13th Child: Legend of the Jersey Devil (film), 84–85
Troy, 13
Twilight (film series), 88

V

Vega, Diego de la, 7
Voltaire, 83

W

Watt, Homer A., 69
Werewolves, 42–43
   in popular culture, 86–88
The Wolfen (Strieber), 87
The Wolfman (film), 87

X

X-Files (TV program), 85

Z

Zorro (Diego de la Vega), 8, 9, 12

PICTURE CREDITS

Cover: © David R. Frazier Photolibrary, Inc./Alamy

© Amblin/Universal/Nelson, Ralph, Jr/ The Kobal Collection/Art Resource, NY, 87

© Andreas Feininger/Time & Life Pictures/Getty Images, 67

© AP Images/Jim Mone, 82

© AP Images/The Register-Herald, Dayton Whittle, 79

© The Art Gallery Collection/Alamy, 22

© Bettmann/Corbis, 37

© Blank Archives/Getty Images, 72, 92

© Buena Vista Pictures/courtesy Everett Collection, 90

© Buyenlarge/Getty Images, 11, 76

© Chris Hellier/Alamy, 38

Dana Nardo, © Gale/Cengage Learning, 4–5

Folk Stories of America: Sea Serpent of Gloucester, Hook, Richard (b.1938)/ Private Collection/© Look and Learn/ The Bridgeman Art Library, 33

© Fotosearch/Getty Images, 65, 68

Francisco Vasquez de Coronado (c.1510-54) Making his Way Across New Mexico, from 'The Great American Explorers', 1905 (oil on canvas), Remington, Frederic (1861-1909)/ Private Collection/The Bridgeman Art Library, 19

© Gale/Cengage Learning, 6-7

© Gary Crabbe/Enlightened Images/ Alamy, 44

Glyph map of Aztec migration from Aztlan to Tenochtitlan, published c.1830 (colour litho), Waldeck, Johann Friedrich Maximilian von (1766-1875) (after)/Newberry Library, Chicago, Illinois, USA/The Bridgeman Art Library, 25

Johnny Appleseed (1774-1847) (coloured engraving), American School, (19th century)/Private Collection/Peter Newark American Pictures/The Bridgeman Art Library, 70

© LOOK Die Bildagentur der Fotografen GmbH/Alamy, 62

© Mary Evans/Ronald Grant/Everett Collection, 83

© MPI/Getty Images, 16

© North Wind/North Wind Picture Archive, 42, 50

© North Wind Picture Archives/Alamy, 29, 56, 59, 60

© Photos 12/Alamy, 53

The Pueblo of Acoma, New Mexico (oil on canvas), Moran, Thomas (1837-1926)/Private Collection/ Peter Newark American Pictures/The Bridgeman Art Library, 14

© RIA Novosti/Photo Researchers, Inc., 41

© Superstock/Everett Collection, 89

© Walt Disney/The Kobal Collection/Art Resource, NY, 81

ABOUT THE AUTHOR

Historian Don Nardo has written numerous acclaimed volumes about ancient and medieval civilizations and peoples. Among these are studies of the religious beliefs and myths of those peoples, including the Greeks, Romans, Egyptians, Sumerians, Celts, Germans, and others. Nardo also composes and arranges orchestral music. He resides with his wife, Christine, in Massachusetts.